MARQUARD
& SEELEY

Also by Noel Hynd

NOVELS

Revenge 1976
The Sadler Inquiry 1978
False Flags 1979
Flowers From Berlin 1985
The Khrushchev Objective 1987
Truman's Spy 1990
Zigzag 1992
Ghosts 1993
A Room for the Dead 1994
Cemetery of Angels 1995

NONFICTION

The Cop and The Kid 1981
The Giants of The Polo Grounds 1988

SCREENPLAYS

Agency 1980
Illegal in Blue 1994
Laura Sent Me Over 1996

MARQUARD
& SEELEY

NOEL HYND

PARNASSUS IMPRINTS
Hyannis, Massachusetts

Parnassus Imprints, Inc.
30 Perseverance Way
Hyannis, MA 02601

Library of Congress Cataloging-in-Publication Data
Hynd, Noel.
    Marquard & Seeley / Noel Hynd. -- 1st ed.
       p.   cm.
    Includes bibliographical references.
    ISBN 0-940160-64-1 (hardcover)
      1. Marquard, Rube, 1889–1980. 2. Pitchers (Baseball)--New York
(N.Y.)--Biography. 3. Pitchers (Baseball)--United States--Biography. 4.
Seeley, Blossom, 1891–1974. 5. Entertainers--United States--Biography.
6. Vaudeville--United States--History.
I. Title
GV865.M346H95   1996
796.357'092--dc20
                                    96-1988
[B]   CIP

Manufactured in the United States of America

This book is especially for
Jeremy Noel Hynd,
my frequent partner in
sports and entertainment.

PREFACE

This is one of the most fascinating baseball and show business stories of the twentieth century. Yet, until now, it has been virtually unknown beyond its own era.

Rube Marquard, young and in his prime, was the quintessential American hero. Young, handsome, and strong, he came out of middle America to star at the most American of all games: baseball. Blossom Seeley, a beautiful young woman from California, rose to stardom in a different field: the American musical theater.

When their lives intersected for a few short scandal-laced years, the emotions generated were white hot. Marquard and Seeley were the DiMaggio and Monroe of their day. It is little wonder that from the very start, their relationship threatened to incinerate itself from its own intensity.

Marquard and Seeley spent the prime years of their young adulthood in an America much different from the one of today. It was the era of the pugnacious Teddy

Roosevelt and the porcine William Howard Taft. An era of ragtime music and low income tax, a time when dollar bills were not only larger format, but went about thirty times as far. An "Indian" was on the U.S. one-cent piece and part of the American West had not yet attained statehood. Much of the country was rigidly segregated at home and the political soul of the nation was still as isolated as it could be in world politics.

The United States was growing, but its growth was only a suggestion of what would eventually occur. New York City was, by 1900, already an immense, crowded metropolis of 5.6 million people, for example, but California was still a state of 1.4 million — slightly fewer inhabitants than South Carolina, and half as many as Texas.

And yet much of what was true in American society at the start of this century remains true today. Actors and athletes were an economic royalty. Those with the talent to entertain — either through the performance of a song or an act, or prowess at executing in a game — was immensely well compensated. If time makes beggars of us all, the ability to entertain has always made princes and princesses of all who had talent in twentieth-century America. Included therein were the men who owned the sporting franchises as well as those who booked the theaters. Theatrical and sporting entrepreneurs built great — almost incomprehensible — fortunes in the "gilded age" just as they do in the present.

It was both a cruel time and an exciting time when Marquard and Seeley were stars of the first rank. Their lives and their attitudes fit perfectly within the context of their time. They were young people with talent and flamboyance. They gravitated to bright lights and excitement the same way they gravitated to scandal. Together, they had the type of romance that most of us could only dream and fantasize about. But rather than dream it, they lived it, for better for worse, and kept it alive for as long as it would last.

This is their story, presented in book form for the first time and recounting primarily the years when they were together. In the pages that follow, they will hopefully step forward out of the past. And the spotlight will shine once again on two uniquely American stars.

For many years I've felt they have merited a curtain call. It is my privilege to have arranged for the venue and the lighting.

Noel Hynd
West Hollywood, California
December 1995

I was in vaudeville for three years, Blossom Seeley and I. That's when she was my wife. . . . I asked her to quit the stage. I told her I could give her everything she wanted.

"No," she said. "Show business is show business."

"Well," I said. "Baseball is mine."

Rube Marquard to Lawrence Ritter in 1966, in The Glory of Their Times

1

$\blacklozenge$

Many years ago there was a comedian named Harry Rose, who called himself "The Broadway Jester." Harry performed in vaudeville and would usually start his act by yelling from offstage, "Here's Harry!"

Then he would enter singing.

One evening the emcee introduced, "Harry Rose, the Broadway Jester." Harry yelled out his familiar "Here's Harry!" and raced on stage.

But this evening the orchestra that accompanied the performers had been moved onto the stage. And the stagehands, perhaps intentionally, had neglected to put into position the wooden runway that would bring Rose over the orchestra pit.

Rose ran out and crashed straight down into the now empty pit. After a moment of stunned silence, the conductor peered down into the pit and asked, "Do you want me to play the introduction again, Harry?"

Somehow the story epitomizes the golden era of vaudeville. It suggests a day when performances were live, yet not so polished that anything couldn't happen.

There was humor, cruelty and irony, jealousy, pain and laughter. Harry Rose was undercut not only by those who should have been supporting him, but also by changing times — the moving of the orchestra onto the stage. And in the end, of course, Rose picked himself up and went on with his performance, that night and other nights, too.

The two most popular forms of entertainment in America during the early part of the twentieth century were live-on-stage theatrical performances and sports. The most popular form of theatrical entertainment was vaudeville — bills of short acts, often as many as ten to twelve to an afternoon or evening. Most acts were song-and-dance or comedy, but there was plenty of room for almost anything people would pay to see. Contortionists. Jugglers. Monologists. Wire walkers. Animal acts and magicians. Famous aviators. And there were really no limits. There was a man named Harry Kahana, who could write upside down, forward or backward, while reading aloud a newspaper story. There were former convicts who came onstage to tell how they "did it." Not far behind them were crime victims who would come onstage and tell how it was done to them.

Some of the acts shake the modern imagination. McNaughton, "The Human Tank," swallowed live frogs, then regurgitated them alive. (The ASPCA soon stopped the act, sparing both the frogs and the audiences.) The Five Gaffney Girls did an act where each "sister" was dressed half-boy, half-girl. They would then perform a dance in such a way that the five girls looked like ten people.

Vasco, "The Mad Musician," played twenty-eight instruments in five minutes. Miss Bird Reeves, champion typist, would type three hundred words per minute while holding a conversation with members of the audience. Howard & Heck were two midgets known as "The Kugelwalker Twins." They came onstage one on the other's shoulders, wearing an overcoat, which made them look like one man of average height until they tossed off the coat and began their act.

Then there were the celebrities who took their turn in the spotlight. Aimee Semple McPherson, the Hollywood evangelist, played the Capitol Theater in New York for $5,000 a week. "She wears a white satin creation, sexy but Episcopalian!" exclaimed the reviewer from *Variety.* In 1910, forty-seven years after Gettysburg, Mrs. LaSalle Corbell Pickett, widow of the famous Confederate General came to the New York stage to recite the poem—you guessed it—*Pickett's Charge.* She received a chilly reception from the Northern audience. A few years later, a notorious accused murderer named Freddie Thompson "performed" in Chicago for $500 a week. Thompson was known as "The Man-Woman," since, at his murder trial (at which he was acquitted) he confessed to having led a simultaneous double life as the wife of a man and the husband of a woman.

There was even a category of entertainment called "dumb acts," not because they were particularly inane (some were) but because they didn't contain dialogue. Dumb acts usually opened a vaudeville bill and closed it, as patrons arriving late or leaving early were prone to make noise. Other members of the audience didn't miss a line because there weren't any. "They see 'em sitting down," it was said of the opening act, and "They see a lot of haircuts," of the closing act.

In their day, "dumb acts" were looked down upon in the United States although they were widely respected in Europe. There's no real explanation for this other than the theory that dumb acts were often acts of skill or performance and took years to perfect, whereas a song or a spoken skit could be learned in a few weeks, if not less. European audiences were said to be more respectful of this. But similarly, many of the dumb acts in the U.S. were performed by Europeans who didn't speak English, and this could have been an element, too.

As usual, there was an irony to this. When vaudeville folded in the U.S., many of the dumb acts caught on with circuses or on tours elsewhere in the world, something spoken acts couldn't do. Moreover, many performers who became stars in later years in America, started as dumb acts in vaudeville. Humorist Fred Allen started as a juggler, as did W.C. Fields. Cary Grant was a stilt walker. Victor McLaglen, who won an Oscar for Best Actor in *The Informer* in 1935, was an "understander" with an acrobatic troop and Burt Lancaster was an acrobat. One of the most successful of all, Tom Mix, America's first cowboy movie star, was a sharpshooter.

Vaudeville was not to be confused with the "legitimate" stage in New York—the straight plays and musicals that played in the big theaters. Nor was it to be confused with the burlesque houses, which put on "naughtier" more risqué shows. While "legit" was considered higher in the social spectrum than burlesque, performers constantly crossed over, although performers who regularly worked the top houses avoided burlesque. But there was always an incentive for getting into vaudeville—salaries were five times as high as legit acting jobs for comparable work. Vo'ville paid big, big bucks. Why else would a man learn how to swallow frogs?

During vaudeville's golden age, the most popular sport in America was baseball, which, as of 1900, had two major leagues, the National and the American, and countless smaller minor leagues stretching in every direction across the country. Boxing was big, also, and so was bicycle racing and track. But baseball, with its American cadences and rhythms, was king. Baseball and vaudeville mirrored each other in this era, both playing the big, booming, rowdy, bustling American cities as well as the smallest, quietest, most God-fearing towns that could clear a diamond in the village square or erect a stage in a storefront.

Baseball and vaudeville, when it played the hinterlands, was pretty much of a lily-white affair, a genuinely "white-bread" operation. In the cities, however, audiences of the "new" Americans, the recent immigrants, found much to amuse themselves both on the vaudeville stages and in the ballparks. Thus, in both, the performers reflected that urban diversity.

Baseball players were not as colorful as the many outlandish vaudeville performers, but the players of the day were a memorable lot, nonetheless. Most were rough-hewn, hard-living, hard-drinking young men who came from city slums and rural farms. Few were well educated and those with a university education in the major leagues could be counted in single digits. Most players were Anglo-Saxon, but many were Irish. There were also Scots, Germans, Italians, Cubans, and Native Americans. Some had physical disabilities. One of the great pitchers of the day, Mordecai "Three Finger" Brown of the Chicago Cubs, owed much of his success—and his nickname—to a threshing machine that maimed and disfigured his throwing hand as a boy. From the maimed hand came 208 wins and 111 losses. Rube Waddell, the fine pitcher for the Philadelphia A's, had a childlike demeanor and liked to chase fire engines—sometimes during games he was pitching. Honus Wagner of the Pittsburgh Pirates, a bandy-legged, awkward-looking kid out of the coal fields of western Pennsylvania, was probably the greatest who ever lived at shortstop, a position defined by quickness and elegance of movement.

Both industries—stage and ballpark—were run by hard-headed businessmen with a cold eye for profit who would quickly be out of business if they didn't sell tickets and refreshments. Some of these men, theater owners and baseball owners, behaved monstrously toward their talent, underpaying them, exploiting them in every imaginable way, and dumping them the moment they were of no further economic value. Many sports and entertainment entrepreneurs became very wealthy and some died broke. It could go either way and everyone knew it.

This was a world much different from our present one, and it was not an easy one in which to stay alive, let alone live comfortably. There was no Social Security, anti-monopoly laws, public housing, voting privileges for women, anti-discrimination laws, or right-to-work laws. There was no radio, television, penicillin, central heating, world wars or air travel. There was no Cy Young Award. But there was a Cy Young.

The country was Protestant by a heavy predominance, and most citizens were of English, Scottish, or German extraction, though another great wave of immigration would soon follow with World War I. There were forty-five states at the turn of the century and the flag had only forty-five stars until Oklahoma added the forty-sixth in November 1907. (New Mexico and Arizona would not complete the "lower forty-eight" until 1912.) The nation's most significant foreign adversary was Mexico, and its most dominating politicians at home were Theodore Roosevelt and William Jennings Bryan.

The heyday of vaudeville was 1908 till 1913, though it was around for at least three decades before that and stumbled along for another two decades until the silent movies and then the "talkies" killed it economically. Like New York, the bustling immigrant city that created it, almost anything one said about "vo'ville" was at least partially true. It was brash, coy, vulgar, sly, witty, exciting, raffish, scurrilous, racist, stupid, brilliant, honest, dishonest, wholesome, and prurient. But above all, it was entertaining.

There were organized circuits in New York and

throughout the country's sleepy hinterlands. By all accounts, the apex of vaudeville was the Palace Theater,
which was built by Martin Beck and opened in 1913 at
Broadway and 47th Street. Having played the Palace in
New York could insure an actor of bookings throughout
the U.S. Never mind that the actor may have struck out—
to borrow a baseball term—at the Palace. The yokels out
in the sticks, booking agents presumed, would never
know the difference. And frequently they didn't. Entertainers walked on and off a red carpet that led to and
from the Palace's stage. Other grand buildings were close
behind in prestige—The Colonial, Hammerstein's
Victoria, the Winter Garden. Some of the buildings and
their names have survived to the present day.

As for the *lowest* rungs of vaudeville, there were many
contenders, but one circuit that went from Salt Lake City,
Utah, to New Orleans, via Montana, may have been the
worst. A nominee for strangest place to play might have
been Gordon & Richard's Comique Theater in Butte,
Montana, where the evening show ran till seven a.m. the
following morning so that local miners could catch the
end of the show, plus buy a shot of booze from management, on their way to work. Yet the arrangement in Butte
wasn't all that strange in the context of the times. Theaters were everywhere, no two alike. In 1910, there were
approximately two thousand small-time vaudeville stages
around the U.S., according to *Variety.* There were scores
in the five boroughs of New York City alone, including
two dozen of the biggest time places in the world.

By modern standards, the times were cruel and so

was the humor. Millions of Americans were both new to their adopted country and new to theater-going. The decorum of the ascot-and-silk hat set that attended Broadway plays was lost on these audiences. Most notorious in their toughness was the crowd at New York's Colonial Theater, which developed a technique of vehement in-unison clapping to drive an unpopular act from the stage. The National Theater in the Bronx was the originating point for "booing" acts that weren't cutting it onstage. Hence the term "Bronx cheer," for the all-American boo. "Rowdyism must stop!" raged *Variety* in 1908, in response to the brutal manners of vaudeville audiences. But it didn't stop and neither did vaudeville.

The vaudeville industry unquestionably mirrored what was happening ethnically in America, both in terms of assimilation and prejudice. When Irish, Italian, German, and Jewish immigrants flooded into New York, each nationality had its own perverse stereotype on stage, usually portrayed in the most demeaning fashion possible — much to the delight of all other ethnic groups. Irish characters were fools who wore ear-to-ear chin beards called "sluggers," couldn't utter a sentence that didn't include the word "begorra," and shamelessly slugged whiskey from flasks. Italian characters were early ill-spoken versions of Chico Marx (who may have perfected the stereotype) and Germans were fat men in blond wigs, who carried heavy pocket watches and had little grasp of English grammar. In the booking agents' parlance of the day, two Italian comedians were known as a "Double Wop act," two Germans were known as a "Double Dutch." There was a black singing group called "The Dark Knights." And so on.

But as these ethnic groups started to prosper in America, changes were taking place. Immigrant societies became more sensitive and booed these stereotypical acts from the stage. They were eventually replaced — sometimes by the same actors — by neater, better-dressed characters who got by on smarts and wit but retained a bit of the Old World accent. Typically, the ethnic group that fared the absolute worst were blacks, who *never* escaped the painfully grotesque racial stereotypes that portrayed them on the vaudeville stage. And there was the added irony of exactly who was portraying or ripping off whom. Black music — songs, ragtime tunes, and minstrel shows — was acceptable to white audiences, but it was even more acceptable if white people performed it. And so they did — in black face, usually applied with a burnt cork. Al Jolson and Eddie Cantor built hugely successful careers by starting off as "burnt cork" men. But lest anyone think that blacks were the only group with their culture ripped off, be aware that the first successful "Jewish Comics," Frank Bush and Sam Curtis, were gentiles.

The ethnic biases and racism in baseball was every bit as straightforward and insidious. Blacks again got the worst of it — they weren't allowed to perform at all. Yet Indians could play (they were invariably called "Chief," as in Chief Meyers of the Giants and Chief Bender of the Athletics), and so could Cubans as long as their skin color wasn't too dark. Many players were Irish, which was fine, since so many Irishmen paid their way into the ballparks. But an Irish player—in the public eye—could rarely aspire to the ideal of Anglo-Saxon Americanism, such as the great Christy Mathewson of the New York Giants.

Sometimes, racial and ethnic bias could take breathtakingly strange turns. In 1901, John J. McGraw, then manager of the Baltimore Orioles in the American League—and who would later manage the New York Giants for thirty years—spotted a player he wanted to sign, a certain Charley Grant who happened to be a black man with straight hair and light brown skin. So McGraw hatched an improbable plan to integrate baseball through subterfuge. He laid plans to sign Grant as "Chief Tokahoma," a Native American. McGraw even went to the trouble of inventing a fake ancestry in the Oklahoma Territory and an ersatz mother living in Kansas. But somehow news of McGraw's scheme leaked out.

"This Cherokee [sic] . . . is really Grant, the crack Negro second baseman, fixed up with war paint and a bunch of feathers," objected Charles Comiskey, President of the Chicago White Sox. "I'll get a Chinaman of my acquaintance and put him on third if McGraw plays this 'Indian.'"

Comiskey then rallied the league president, Ban Johnson, and other club owners. Thus went integration down the tubes for another half century. Few white Americans saw anything wrong with this. As recently as 1896, the U.S. Supreme Court had ruled that "separate but equal" was a legal and fair doctrine. And though few people would come right out and say it, there was a national consensus that Protestant was socially superior to Catholic, both were better than Jewish, and white was in all ways superior to black. Entertainment reflected this, both on the stage and on the athletic field.

In baseball, like vaudeville, even nicknames — by modern standards — could be cruel beyond belief. Luther Taylor, a deaf mute (and probably mentally retarded) who pitched for the Giants from 1900 till 1908, was nicknamed Dummy. At least he never heard anyone call him that. And his contribution to major league baseball may have been the finger signals that Roger Bresnahan, his catcher, devised to indicate which pitch to throw. One finger, fastball and two fingers, curve, was thus born.

In November 1895, theater entrepreneur Oscar Hammerstein made a bold move by opening the gargantuan Olympia Theater on Broadway between Forty-fourth and Forty-fifth streets.

The arrival of the Olympia was a portent for the development of what had been known as Longacre Square as a theatrical center. At the cavernous Olympia, a half-dollar ticket bought admission to a collection of entertainments all under one roof — a theater, a concert hall, bowling alleys, a billiard hall, a smoking lounge, and a Turkish bath, all topped by a roof garden. The interior, in stucco and punctuated with statues, was in a style attributed — perhaps loosely — to the Bourbon kings of France. The music hall itself was a "gilded age" special. It was said to be in the mode of Louis Quatorze: a white and gold motif, with ornamented walls, paneled ceilings decorated with floral designs, and a massive chandelier hanging from a rosette surrounded by dancing Cupids. To a modern observer, this may have been more evocative of early King Farouk than Late Louis Quatorze.

Opening the Olympia was a spectacular move, but its economics, for Hammerstein at least, were shaky. The Olympia failed to show a profit in its first three years and was ultimately mortgaged to Marc Klaw and A.L. Erlanger of the legitimate theater syndicate that bore their names. The latter must have hated his given name as he was always called "A.L."

Klaw and Erlanger eventually sold the building to Marcus Loew, a vaudeville magnate. But Hammerstein's decision to build signaled a commitment to the area, a commitment that would work out better for others who followed. Eventually, Oscar's nephew Willie Hammerstein opened his Victoria at Forty-second Street and Seventh Avenue and the Palace would go up at Broadway and Forty-seventh Street. All of these theaters were considered houses of moderate size—approximately two thousand seats. And right nearby sat the Hippodrome, the grandest house of all in terms of seating capacity, with a massive 6,100 seats. (Today, on that location at Forty-fourth Street and Sixth Avenue sits one of the most ironically named buildings in Manhattan—the Hippodrome Parking garage.)

Two other factors helped immeasurably in building

and settling the area for theaters. In 1904—only a few months after the Wright Brothers' 120-foot, twelve-second flight at Kitty Hawk, North Carolina—New York City opened its first subway, the Interborough line. The railroad entered Manhattan via the twenty-year-old Brooklyn Bridge, proceeded north along Manhattan's east side, then headed west on Forty-second Street before turning north on Broadway to continue uptown on the West Side. Shortly thereafter, the *New York Times* opened a new building at the precise intersection where the subway turned north. The intersection thus acquired a new name: Times Square. That same subway line, and others that would follow, would soon bring millions of customers a year to what became the new center of theater, vaudeville, and entertainment in America's largest city. It was the nightly concentration of electric lights in this area that caused the section of Manhattan to first be called "the Great White Way."

It was also in this section of the city where the world of sports and the world of theatrical entertainment coalesced. There had been close links between people in the two worlds before. In the 1880s a tall, articulate star ballplayer for the New York Giants, John Montgomery Ward, had a much publicized romance with one Helen Dauvray, a Broadway actress and one of the great beauties of her day. Ward was constantly seen on evenings in the wings of the legitimate theaters waiting for La Dauvray to finish her performance. Then the two would go out on the town, sometimes till five a.m., much to the delight of Broadway gossips and scandal sheets. (Unlike many highly publicized romances, this one ended in marriage.) A frequent stopping place for Ward and Dauvray was a restaurant called The Old Home Plate at 16 West 27th Street in Manhattan. The restaurant, named with an intentional metaphor between baseball and good, hearty, home-style cooking, became a favorite of theater people and the sporting crowd. A similar fusion occurred in the 1900s as the vaudeville stage grew in popularity and baseball expanded from one major league to two.

John McGraw was instrumental in the link. He, along with an elfin jockey named Tod Sloan, owned pool halls in New York. The pool halls drew Broadway people and McGraw began making contacts. After the New York Giants won the National League pennant in 1904—and subsequently refused to dignify the American League by playing their champion Boston club—a huge celebration was held to mark the first baseball championship of the twentieth century in New York. The celebration was a "benefit" for the Giants players and was held at the Klaw-Erlanger theater at 45th and Broadway. Tickets were sold to the public, with a portion of the receipts going to the players and the rest, it was rumored, to further line the pockets of John T. Brush, the Giants owner.)

Tod Sloan was the master of ceremonies. Louis Mann, one of the great stage actors of the day, presented McGraw with a pair of diamond-studded cuff links. Joe Humphries, a young Madison Square Garden sports announcer said to have "a silver voice," presented a large loving cup to the entire Giants team. Other renowned actors, including Digby Bell, Dan McAvoy, and Gus

Edwards, presented baseball-oriented vaudeville skits, teaming with two lovely actresses named Grace Cameron and Helen Byron.

Here was an event that brought together the world of Broadway, that lived and worked along the Great White Way, and the world of New York sports, which was centered around the Polo Grounds several miles uptown at Eighth Avenue and 155th Street. It set the stage, with John McGraw's first great New York teams in the offing, for the Giants to capture the hearts of the city. And it prepared the way for the story of a young Giant pitcher named Rube Marquard and a young star stage actress named Blossom Seeley to be possible.

2

◆

The life of Rube Marquard, which was to span nine-tenths of a century, began in a resolutely middle-class neighborhood in Cleveland, Ohio, on October 9, 1889. Marquard was born Richard LeMarquis. His father was the chief civil engineer of the city of Cleveland and years later, when recalling their stormy relationship, Marquard would refer to him — with a mixture of affection, respect, and disdain — as a "professional man."

There were five children in the family, four brothers including Richard and one sister. LeMarquis senior had hopes that the boys would become professional people like their father — teachers, doctors and lawyers. Such was not to be the case, and therein lay one of the central conflicts of Rube Marquard's life. Spending time in school, reading and studying was not Rube's idea of having fun. Only one thing was: baseball. It might be said that baseball was Marquard's first, final, and ultimate love.

"I told my mother when I was six that I wanted to be a ballplayer and that one day I'd show her what I could do on the field," Marquard told an interviewer late in his life. "She died the next year and never got to see me play. My dad . . . never liked baseball. When I told him that I wanted to be a ballplayer he just looked at me and said, 'So, you want to be a bum for the rest of your life.'"

"'If I'm going to be a bum,' I told him, 'then I'll be a good bum. If I'm bad, I won't go that far.'"

Indeed, the chasm of understanding—or lack of it—was profound between young Richard and his father. Baseball players were widely held in low social esteem at this time in America. The elder LeMarquis could barely believe that they were paid to play a game, though his son correctly insisted that they were.

"Don't get me wrong," Rube said not long before his ninetieth birthday, looking back upon a life that had been more than full. "I was a good student and could have gone to college. I just didn't want to. Baseball was what I wanted and I was fortunate enough to be good at it."

The arguments used to go round and round in the LeMarquis household. Young Richard's paternal grandfather, who had emigrated to America from France, would frequently take his grandson's side, citing the fact that he had wanted his own son—Richard's father—to become a stone cutter as he had been. But the father had become a civil engineer instead.

"Give him a chance and see what he can do," Granddad LeMarquis would tell his son.

"But Dad would never listen," Rube would recall. "'Ballplayers are no good,' he'd say, 'and they will never be any good.'" But baseball was what Rube wanted. And baseball was what he would get. A lifetime of it.

As a boy, Marquard was tall and lanky, much the same physique that he would eventually bring to the National League when he was a grown man. As a player later with the New York Giants, he stood six feet three, a veritable giant (small 'g') in a day when many players were between five foot eight and five foot ten. Christy Mathewson, the famous "Big Six," who was Marquard's boyhood idol, was commonly accepted to be tall and regal, and Marquard in most pictures appears to be an inch and a half taller than Christy. Marquard, as an adult, also never tired of noting that his sister, who stood six foot two as an adult, was the shortest of the five LeMarquis siblings.

As a boy, the gangly Richard hung around with the older kids and played ball with them. Many of them didn't even realize how much younger he was. He gravitated to the pickup games that were common in town squares of Middle America at the turn of the last century, and soon one thing led to another. In the America of the early 1900s, where baseball occupied a central part of American culture, the top amateurs in a town often knew the local minor league players. And the minor leaguers usually knew someone who had made it to the majors.

Some two decades later, Governor Alfred E. Smith of New York, eventually the Democratic candidate for President in 1928, was once asked by a young boy how a fellow got into politics.

"Son," Smith replied, "just by hanging around."

A young man with talent, as Richard had, could make his way into baseball in much the same way.

By the time Richard was thirteen he found a way to

make himself useful, get an inside shot at baseball, and meet the players at the same time. The American League was a new major league in 1901 and Cleveland had a charter franchise, having two years earlier escaped the purgatory of the National League's lower depths. It will not be forgotten that Cleveland baseball hit its all-time low with the infamous 20-134 Cleveland Spiders of 1899, the last year the city played in the twelve-team National League.

The Cleveland club in the American League was not called the Indians just yet. They were called the Blues and then, increasingly after 1902, the Naps, so-named after their young star, Napoleon Lajoie, whom a spiteful Connie Mack had sold to Cleveland after a contract squabble. When the American League season ended, and as long as the weather stayed reasonable, many of the Cleveland players would barnstorm around the area. The players needed a batboy. Richard volunteered.

Several things came together at this point. Young Richard remained smitten with the game. And he started to make contacts. A friend named Howard Wakefield — five years his senior — from pickup games around Cleveland, had already made the minor leagues. And the Naps' third baseman, another Cleveland native named William "Boo" Bradley, had a barnstorming team of his own known as the Boo Gang. Bradley, who had a long and solid major league career from 1899 through 1915, took a liking to Richard and even let him pitch a few games. Richard was a tall, strong left-hander, a detail lost on no one. In the pickup games, he threw hard enough to begin impressing eyewitnesses.

"So by the time I was fifteen or sixteen I knew a lot of ball players," Marquard told Lawrence Ritter in *The Glory of Their Times* in 1966. "And I had my heart set on being a Big Leaguer myself."

In the summer of 1906, five years into the presidency of the first Roosevelt, Richard received a letter from his friend Howard Wakefield. Wakefield was dividing his time that season catching for Waterloo of the Iowa State League and for Washington in the American League. He was, however, with Waterloo when he wrote to Richard.

"We can use a good left-handed pitcher," the letter said. "And if you come to Waterloo, I'll recommend you to the manager."

Imagine the young man's elation. Then imagine the horror when Richard pictured his father's reaction. But without money from his father, how would Richard get to Waterloo from Cleveland?

Richard exchanged letters and telegrams with the Waterloo club and its manager, a man whom Marquard would remember years later only as "Mr. Frisbee." Frisbee, was very likely an Iowan named Charlie Frisbee, who'd played a handful of games in the National League in 1899 and 1900.

The discussion went back and forth about expense money to get to Waterloo, but the minor league management was pinching its pennies so tightly that the Indian upon them would probably have yelped. No money was forthcoming. Then three weeks passed and the opportunity to pitch for Waterloo seemed to be slipping away. So

Richard made a decision that would alter his life. He would run away to play baseball.

"I was sixteen years old and had never been away from home before," Marquard recalled years later. "It took me five days and five nights, riding freight trains, sleeping in open fields, hitching rides any way I could. My money ran out the third day, and after that I ate when and how I could."

Eventually, Marquard found his way to the Illinois Central station in Waterloo. From there, he found Howard Wakefield playing billiards in the back room of a none-too-charming pool hall. Wakefield introduced the young southpaw to Mr. Frisbee and the manager penciled in a start for Richard LeMarquis against Keokuk.

Marquard pitched and won the game either 6–1 or 6–2, depending on which account of the contest one wishes to believe. Richard then asked for a contract.

"Keokuk is in last place," Frisbee answered. "Wait till Oskaloosa comes in this weekend. They're in second place. If you can beat them, then we'll talk."

Marquard lost his second start and Waterloo management offered neither a contract nor expense money.

"I felt cheated," Richard recalled. "The whole experience soured me on baseball, and taught me that you couldn't trust baseball owners."

So at age sixteen Richard rode the rails like a hobo for the second time in a month. A few miles outside of Chicago, he jumped off a moving freight train to avoid railroad company detectives. Then he set out on foot, eventually wandering into a local fire house. A group of suburban Chicago smoke eaters befriended the young man, fed him and gave him some expense money, enabling him to return home to Cleveland, wiser and disillusioned.

But not completely disenchanted.

Richard hung around Cleveland for the rest of that summer, rarely missing a possible pickup game and frequently ruminating on the way he had been treated in his brief appearance in professional baseball. By the time the next summer came around, Richard was still pitching. But he also had an "honest job."

In what might have been some weird combination of boyish dreams, Richard began working for an ice cream company and also pitching in an industrial league. The two jobs were not unrelated. The company's name was either the Fanning Ice Cream Company or the Telling Ice Cream Company. Long afterward, Marquard could never remember exactly which. What he clearly remembered, however, was the pay scale. Twenty-five dollars a week — $15 for checking the cans on the company wagon when the horses pulled it away, and an extra $10 to pitch for the company ball club each Sunday.

Richard's ego was having no problem at this time. He was the standout pitcher in the semipro league and, while few written records were kept, most accounts had it that the young lefty mowed down the opposition fairly regularly. That was, of course, how Marquard would recall it. "I hardly lost a game," he observed years later. And he probably didn't.

This was also one of Richard's last gasps at what was then considered "amateurism." He set down opponents so deftly in the warehouse-and-foundry circuit that local scouts couldn't fail to notice. Eventually, scouts from the Cleveland major league team summoned him to their office situated at League Park at 66th Street and Lexington Avenue.

Cleveland offered Richard one hundred dollars a month to play minor league baseball and termed it "a wonderful offer."

A dream come true. Right?

Wrong.

Obviously, the ice cream had left a better taste in the seventeen-year-old's mouth than the Iowa State League had.

"I make that much right now from the ice cream company," Marquard answered, thinking back on the previous summer in Iowa. "I've been taken advantage of before and it's not going to happen again."

The Cleveland club attempted to talk Richard into signing, but wouldn't improve their dollar offer. Richard wouldn't lower his price and walked out of League Park.

On his way home, however, he stopped at a sporting goods store at 724 Prospect Avenue. The store was owned by Boo Bradley of the Naps and his partner, Charlie Carr. Carr was a former journeyman major leaguer who was currently playing first base and managing for Indianapolis of the American Association. Carr was surprised that Cleveland had failed to sign the local standout.

"How would you like to sign with me?" Carr asked.

"If a major league club won't pay me what I want, how could you do it?" Richard asked.

"How much do you want?"

Marquard held his breath and went for two hundred dollars a month. Carr expressed shock, then agreed to Richard's price.

"Then and there," Marquard later recalled, "I signed my first professional contract."

It should have been a joyous occasion. But Carr wanted Richard to report immediately, which meant Richard had to thrash out the matter with his father that evening. "Oh, that was a terrible night," Marquard would remember.

"I've told you time and time again that I don't want you to become a professional ballplayer," LeMarquis Senior said. "But you've made your mind up. Now I'm going to tell you something: when you cross that threshold, don't come back. I don't ever want to see you again."

"You don't mean that, Dad," the young man replied.

"Yes, I do."

"Well, I'm going, and some day you'll be proud of me."

With those words, Richard LeMarquis left home three months short of his eighteenth birthday. He would not see his father again for more than a decade.

Indianapolis optioned the young man to Canton of the Central League, where he quickly learned how to become a professional ballplayer. The blazing speed that he had shown in the industrial league around Cleveland proved almost as baffling to hitters at the Double A level. It wasn't that he "hardly ever" lost a game, because he lost thirteen. But he also won twenty-three games in forty appearances, a total that led the league. It was an auspicious start. Already, Richard was pitching better than his level of pro ball. The performance also gained him a promotion to Indianapolis for 1908.

As it happened, spring training the following year was in French Lick, Indiana. And, as it further happened, the first opponent of the Indianapolis club was the Cleveland Naps.

Several of the Cleveland players ("the whole bunch that I used to carry bats for," Marquard remembered) recognized the young lefty as he was warming up.

"What are you doing here?" some of them yelled. "Are you the batboy?"

"No," Richard answered, "I'm going to pitch against you today. And I'm going to beat you, too."

"You couldn't beat a drum," someone answered.

Boo Bradley and a couple of the other Cleveland players privately came over to wish Richard well. Then the young Indianapolis hurler settled in and thoroughly baffled his hometown team, shutting them out, 2–0. After the game, the Cleveland team offered to buy Richard's contract for $3,500. But Indianapolis refused the offer and kept Marquard for the season.

"Don't worry," a representative of the Indianapolis club said to Richard, in a bizarre moment of labor-management candor. "I won't sell you right now. Later on, I'll be able to sell you for a lot more."

And as the season progressed, success continued. By midsummer, Marquard was 14–6 with an ERA of 1.58 and six shutouts. He found himself opposing another hot rookie, young Smoky Joe Wood of the Kansas City Blues, who would also soon burst into the major leagues. Richard, however, was hardly intimidated. He was 37–19 now in his pro career and found himself not lacking in confidence.

"If I was you, I wouldn't warm up now," he taunted Wood. "I'm gonna beat you."

Wood was just as hot, but Richard LeMarquis outpitched him, 2–1. That same day, when a sportswriter noticed Rube's physical resemblance to the great Rube Waddell, Connie Mack's flaky liquor-besotted southpaw ace with the Philadelphia Athletics, the young Indianapolis hurler found himself with the same nickname — Rube. During this time, the "LeMarquis" name was being systematically massacred in box scores as "Marquard." And the name stuck.

Within a few weeks, Richard LeMarquis, who had learned how to pitch winning baseball, had also been transformed into "Rube Marquard." When Rube started getting mail, telegrams, and inquiries from scouts addressed to "R. Marquard" of the Indianapolis club, he made no effort to correct anyone. Rather than mess with a good thing, Richard LeMarquis adopted the new name. Like Caesar, the honor had been thrust upon him.

"Originally," he laughed many years later, "they added a 't' to my name, also. Richard Marquardt. But the newspapers kept dropping it, so I dropped it, too."

Rube blazed his way through the American Association that summer of 1908. He had the scouts salivating. Not yet nineteen years old, he neared the end of a season in which he would lead the league in games, 47, innings pitched, 367, and wins, 28. He was big, strong, handsome, young, overpowering, full of himself and, best of all, a left-hander.

Indianapolis announced that they would showcase Marquard on September 5, the end of their season, against the Columbus club in Indianapolis. Scouts from just about every major league team were there. Rube responded by tossing either a no-hitter or a perfect game, depending on whose account one wishes to believe. In any case, the scouts knew what they had seen, and they liked it.

The New York Giants, the Philadelphia Athletics, and the Boston Pilgrims were perhaps the most successful clubs in the two major leagues. But the Giants had the most cash. They also had a skipper in John McGraw who would stop at nothing to get the players he wanted.

The Cleveland team was in the Marquard sweepstakes, too, anxious to sign a hometown boy and equally anxious not to let the same hometown boy get away twice.

So Cleveland entered the bidding and went as high as $10,500. John McGraw was having none of that, however, and his emissary bid $11,000. There the bidding stopped. The Giants had the young pitcher.

In acquiring Rube Marquard, the New York Giants also acquired some headlines. The sum was unprecedented at the time, more, by far, than any club had ever paid to acquire a young player. Three years earlier, for example, the Detroit Tigers had paid only $700 to purchase the now batting champion Ty Cobb from Augusta. In 1909, the Giants would pay their great hurler and national idol, Christy Mathewson, a flat $10,000, while Cobb would eventually sign a three-year contract at $9,000 per annum. So $11,000, be it salary or purchase, was a princely — if not a kingly — sum to throw in any direction for talent that was unproven at the major league level.

And Marquard would not be allowed to forget it.

The newspapers in New York quickly dubbed Rube "the $11,000 Beauty," even though his rookie salary would only be about $800 per year. Newspapers trumpeted his imminent arrival in the city and fans anxiously waited for his first start. In modern terms, the Marquard transaction might have been equal to buying an untested player for $3.5 million.

No doubt there was plenty of resentment among the players, many of whom made two to three thousand dollars per year. The resentment was perhaps best illustrated when Marquard first arrived in New York a few days after his signing in Indianapolis.

Marquard appeared at the Giants clubhouse and, for all his midwest bravado, was somehow intimidated. Instead of opening the door, he knocked.

A gruff-voiced Giant outfielder named Cy Seymour, who had been a regular for McGraw that year, opened the door.

"Who the hell are you?" Seymour asked.

"Rube Marquard," was the answer.

Seymour held a contemptuous eye to the youngster. Another player, Mike Donlin, loomed into the doorway behind Seymour. His gaze was equally critical. Then Donlin turned.

"Hey, fellows!" Donlin barked. "Look at this bum McGraw just paid $11,000 for!"

With this auspicious start, Marquard was allowed into the clubhouse. And things did not improve all that rapidly. McGraw knew that the jump from the American Association to the National League could be a harsh one, so the skipper had already announced that he planned to keep the kid primarily on the bench, "so he can learn the hitters." Marquard was also the youngest man on the club. Only Fred Merkle at age nineteen, and Doc Crandall, at twenty, were close. Most of McGraw's veterans were in their late twenties or early thirties. Mathewson, for example, was twenty-eight.

And then there were the pressures of the pennant race.

On September 23, 1908, one of baseball's most famous games was played at the Polo Grounds. With Marquard sitting near McGraw, the Giants played the Cubs in the famous 1–1 tie in which the young, inexperienced Fred Merkle was called out for failing to run to second base following Al Bridwell's single into the outfield. The hit would have won the game for New York. When the game was replayed at the end of the season, Chicago won and nipped the pennant from New York by one game.

Historians have forever failed to note, however, that the very next day, against Cincinnati at the Polo Grounds, Marquard made his major league debut.

McGraw probably would have held back the eighteen-year-old until the following spring, but management, in the person of owner John Brush, was anxious to showcase his investment for the fans. As it turned out, McGraw had known what he was doing.

Marquard was as jittery as a dozen frightened cats when he took the mound for the first time in the National League. So frightened that he plunked the first batter with a wayward pitch. Then he walked the next two men he faced.

Rube, facing the Reds' best hitter in Hans Lobert, then beckoned to his catcher, Roger Bresnahan. "Maybe I'm trying too hard," Rube suggested. "Maybe I should take something off the next pitch."

"Okay," replied Bresnahan. "But don't take off too much or this guy will bust one."

Marquard proceeded to take off exactly too much. Lobert powered the ball over the left field wall of the Polo Grounds for a grand slam, the ball rolling into the gritty railroad yards that stood across the street from the ballpark. The first four major league hitters Marquard would face all scored.

The fans were quick to let everyone know what they thought of their "$11,000 Beauty," booing and hooting raucously at the young pitcher. And yet actually, though the outing was always recalled as a bad one, Marquard settled down a bit, allowing five more hits and only one more run over five full innings. He took the loss as well as much heat from the spectators when he left the game. Yet, even under these trying circumstances, his self-confidence showed signs of returning. Reporters on the scene reported the torrent of disapproval that cascaded down upon Rube when he left the game, but also noted that he left the field "waving confidently to the bleacherites."

A better outing would have made a better story and certainly would have left a fonder memory. But the fact was, Rube was finally in the major leagues. And not just the major leagues. He was in *New York*.

A few years earlier, a Giant teammate, Larry Doyle, an amiable high-spirited shortstop whom the writers called "Laughing Larry," had coined a phrase that would be reworked many times in sports over the years.

"Goddamn!" Doyle had remarked when the Giants had been on one of their king-size rolls through the National League. "It's great to be young and a New York Giant."

It wouldn't be long before Rube Marquard would know exactly what Laughing Larry had meant.

3

———◆———

San Francisco, California, in 1891 was still in many ways the West Coast boomtown that it had become in the late 1840s. Until the discovery of gold at nearby Sutter's Creek in 1848, San Francisco wasn't much more than a remote little fishing settlement that had been founded by the Spaniards in 1776.

But by 1850, the Enclave by the Bay was on its way to becoming the City by the Bay, its population leaping from 500 to 30,000, perhaps one of the fastest percentage gains in population in American urban history. A "western Wall Street" grew as millions of dollars' worth of gold was either panned from rivers or blasted out of the hills by dynamite. The Pacific shipping trade increased via the fleets of merchant vessels that lined San Francisco harbor, and the city's economic base solidified even more.

By the last decade of the century, the three most salient characteristics of San Francisco were known the world around. The fog, of course, had always been there. But now came the stately Victorian houses and the cable cars. One noteworthy visitor to San Francisco in 1882, Robert

Louis Stevenson, called Nob Hill "the hill of palaces" after the Victorian mansions built there. Seven years later, another visiting author, Rudyard Kipling, perhaps when dodging for the safety of the sidewalk, noted that the cable cars "turn corners at right angles, cross each other's lines, and for all I know, may run up the sides of houses."

Blossom Seeley was reportedly born in this city and into its boomtown environment on July 16, 1891. It was an atmosphere in which a person could go just as far as his or her smarts or talents could take him.

Blossom started early.

As a schoolgirl, her parents put her on the stage where she would sing and dance. She was born with the name Minnie Guyer but as a child performer took the billing of "The Little Blossom" or just "Little Blossom." By age ten she had already selected a first name that would stay with her for a lifetime, although exactly where the "Seeley" came from will probably never be known.

There lived in San Francisco of that era a showman named D.J. Grauman, whose temperament surely matched that of his adopted city. Grauman was a transplanted Southerner, from Louisville, Kentucky. He was a heavily featured man with a shrewd but good-natured face. His hair was white by the turn of the century and was frequently compared to a powder puff.

Grauman, though based in the West, had a huge influence in American show business, and not simply because his son, the famous Sid Grauman, eventually founded the world famous Chinese Theater in Los Angeles, a temple which still exists today in Hollywood, famous as much for the concrete friezes of celebrity hands and feet in the sidewalk, as for any entertainment it now shows.

D.J. Grauman, also known as Pop Grauman, took the first "colored minstrels" on the road after the Civil War. When he came to San Francisco, he was also the first to introduce quality vaudeville to San Francisco audiences for a dime admission. He was also a man known as being particularly kind and considerate of performers in a business that was notorious for the opposite.

Happily, D.J. Grauman was well rewarded by the business he treated so well. His Unique Theater in San Francisco (later renamed Grauman's National) was usually packed even without the newspaper or billboard advertising favored by competitors. By 1909, Pop Grauman was so well known in San Francisco that he ran for mayor. Unfortunately, most voters felt he belonged right where he was—producing shows. He lost the election.

Interestingly, D.J. Grauman had succeeded by taking the high road in the entertainment business. His theater, which stood at 7th and Market streets, was said to be the home of "polite vaudeville." Audiences of the day knew exactly what that meant.

"If I'd had listened to other people I'd never have made a success of this business," Grauman told the San Francisco *Examiner* in 1903. "Everybody said that I'd never make a success of this place unless I allowed smoking and drinking and catered generally to the Bohemian element. But I have demonstrated that there are more respectable people than Bohemians. I don't allow smoking or drinking, or vulgarity on the stage. And I never even allow an intoxicated person into my house."

It was a prescription for clean entertainment for general audiences. Just as organized baseball had suffered from rowdy ill-behaved fans in the 1880s and 1890s — the American League had been conceived as a civilized alternative to the rowdiness of the National League — polite vaudeville worked a segment of the audience that rejected the more risqué off-color forms of entertainment. A Grauman theater, in other words, was the type of place a man could bring his family. It was the type of place a child performer could play.

And did.

In 1906, on the eve of the big earthquake that eventually — along with the fire that followed it — leveled much of the city, Grauman wandered into a small cafe where "Little Blossom" was playing. She sang two songs: "Teasin' Rag" and "A Dollar And Thirty Cents." Grauman was so impressed that he booked her for a week at his theater. He also offered her a suggestion on her singing style that would stay with her for the rest of her life: Make every man in the audience feel as if she was singing directly to him.

When Blossom made her debut at Grauman's in San Francisco, she was billed as "Little Blossom — the Vivacious Comedienne." She was, as mentioned, not new to the stage, having made her professional debut at a local cafe at age ten. She was both cute — short hair, short white dress, a pink ribbon around her waist — and precocious. At age twelve, to the accompaniment of a single piano, she had belted out (with "a huge voice of watermelon luciousness," noted one local reviewer) a song called "My Ragtime Joe." Then, to cool things off emotionally a bit, she sang another ragtime tune, this one titled "Chicken." Surprisingly enough, the song was about a chicken.

Some of Seeley's early material would seem racist by today's standards. And much of vaudeville entertainment was cruel — as noted earlier — in terms of sex and race. In the first decade of the twentieth century it was perfectly fair game, for example, to make ethnic jokes and slurs in the midst of an otherwise upstanding act. The Irish took a pretty good hosing. (A sample: What would an Irishman do if he won the lottery? Answer: Buy a pick with a longer handle.) But since they were the immigrant group that spoke English most readily, Irish comedians sprung up who would tell Irish jokes to Irish audiences, thus some-what negating the slurs. But blacks came in for the cruel-est humor and, to make matters worse, their finest cul-tural contributions were freely ripped off. Ragtime music was now coming out of the black piano parlors of Kansas City and St. Louis and was quickly co-opted for white audiences as soon as it became borderline acceptable. Which brings us back to Seeley's earliest material, and a form of entertainment called "coon shouting."

Seeley as a teenager helped popularize a method of taking a "Negro" tune, singing it with a syncopated rag-time beat and belting it out with a big voice. Sometimes this was done in a comic — which is to say, racially pejo-rative — manner. Two stars of the stage from the late nine-teenth century, Fay Templeton and May Irwin, had polished, successful acts of this sort and were obvious influences upon young Blossom. For several years, in fact, Blossom would perform many of the same songs as the highly successful May Irwin, so much so that the newspapers, while calling Seeley "wholesome and ingenuous" also referred to her, in a favorable way, as "the pocket edition of May Irwin." However, as Seeley hit her late teens and grew from a girl into a woman, the "pocket edition" euphemism was quickly forgotten.

By 1903, the San Francisco *Examiner* proclaimed Seeley "the Queen of Grauman's," and clearly, judging by the audience reactions of the day, she was what audiences were coming to Grauman's to see.

Very quickly, her reputation spread on the West Coast. Her booking agent found offers for her in other houses in California and by 1907 and 1908 she was playing respectable burlesque houses as far south as Los Angeles. During the winter-spring season of 1908–1909, she played a successful engagement of thirty-eight straight weeks at a vaudeville house in Los Angeles, where she became one of the top stage stars to date in that city. But by fall of 1909, she had taken her act north to San Francisco again, where she did a ten-minute vaudeville act at a theater called the Wigwam, one of the top venues in San Francisco. She did songs, notably a new one called "Put Your Arms Around Me, Honey," and told what were referred to as Negro dialect stories. Her reviews and audiences were excellent.

But it was back in Los Angeles in 1910 that a talent scout spotted her for the famous variety team of Weber and Fields. Lew Weber, in addition to doing a "Double Dutch" act with his partner Joe Fields, was heavily into big lavish musicals. And in Seeley he spotted someone who could play an essential ingredient as the soubret (or soubrette), a saucy coquettish young maiden — a role borrowed from the comic operas of Europe of the previous century.

It was a role that Seeley was ready for, both onstage and off. And, it was a role that would carry her to stardom. Yet just as significant in her life was another event that transpired in the summer of 1910. She met a man named Joe Kane, an actor from New York (via Pittsburgh) who would take more than a passing interest in her career, as well as the personal direction of her life.

In a related development that would also affect Seeley's career and life, baseball and show business were beginning to intertwine very neatly. True, going back to the 1880s, as noted, John Montgomery Ward had provided a major link when he married Helen Dauvray. Mike King Kelly had made some personal appearances, as did Cap Anson. And a stand-up monologist named De Wolf Hopper made a living for several decades out of an overbearing recital of the Ernest Thayer poem *Casey At The Bat*. But in the first years of the twentieth century, as the entertainment industry had developed in New York, boxers and wrestlers began making the transition from the sports box office to the theater box office.

John L. Sullivan, Bob Fitzsimmons, and "Gentleman Jim" Corbett were all heavyweight champs who starred on the vaudeville stage. True, these appearances were billed kindly as "special attractions" and no one expected these big muscular guys to start swiping roles from the Booths or the Barrymores. But sometimes there were surprises. Jim Corbett, for example, really could act. He proved this in several stage appearances, but most notably in a play called *Cashel Byron's Profession* at Daly's Theater on Broadway in 1906.

One of the leading Broadway impresarios of the day was Willie Hammerstein (uncle of Oscar Hammerstein who years later, along with Richard Rogers, composed such Broadway hits as *South Pacific*). Willie Hammerstein booked more champion athletes than any other theater manager, and for a good reason. Hammerstein knew that at least three-quarters of the audiences at his theater came from the "sporting element" of New York City. They jammed the joint to see a winner up close and in person. Hammerstein refined this to such an art form that there was eventually a standard joke in New York sporting circles that when someone won a big athletic event — baseball, biking, boxing, rowing, or track — his business manager would say to him, "Hurry up, take a shower and put on a suit. You're booked at Hammerstein's this evening." Decades later, the Broadway wise guy, Ed Sullivan, would use the technique on television with the "We have in our audience tonight, the pitcher who, this afternoon with the New York Yankees . . . ."

The practice probably hit full stride for baseball players in 1908 with the New York Giants outfielder named Mike Donlin, the same player who had given, along with

Cy Seymour, young Rube Marquard a tough time upon his first arrival at the Giants clubhouse. Donlin was a tough, wiry Irishman from Erie, Pennsylvania, who could do a lot of things very well. Drinking, fighting, acting, getting arrested, romancing great-looking women, and playing baseball were perhaps his best six. And Mike, having some pretty good smarts in addition to his charm and athletic ability, sometimes found ways to do the first five practically simultaneously.

Not all of Donlin's relationships with show business people were particularly favorable. In 1903 in Baltimore, Donlin, who had played for Cincinnati that year, was named in a criminal complaint for assaulting an actress named Mabel Fields and her escort, Ernest Slayton. Donlin pleaded guilty, claiming that he had been drunk at the time and had little recollection of what he had done. As a sympathy plea, the excuse fell on deaf judicial ears. The court sentenced Donlin to a $250 fine, which he paid, and a six-month jail sentence, which he served. Donlin came back the next year to hit .351 for Cincinnati. John McGraw purchased his contract from the Reds in July of 1904, bringing to the Giants a fine hitter and — ultimately — a major headache. Donlin quickly became a solid star in New York, hitting third in the batting order and playing as the regular centerfielder for John McGraw's first great championship team, the 1905 Giants. Donlin hit .356, led the league in runs, then led his team in runs and hits in the World Series.

It should be noted here that the era under discussion was one in which nighttime baseball did not yet exist at

the major league level, even as a dream of the future.
Ballplayers reported to their parks by nine or ten in the
morning. Games usually began around three o'clock in
the afternoon and were usually over by five or soon afterward. That meant that a player's free time came in
the evening—always the Devil's Workshop for young
men in lively metropolitan areas.

Donlin would have been a first-rate carouser in Amish
country, but in New York he rose to Olympian propor-
tions. His afterdark escapades soon put him in contact
with numerous big-time show business people, not the
least of which was a small-statured but lovely young actress named Mabel Hite. Mabel was a successful stage
woman who had an excellent career as a singer-comedi-
enne before meeting Donlin. Naturally, Mabel knew producers and the producers were more than anxious to talk
to Mike. So Donlin and Hite formed an act both on and
off stage, the latter of which resulted in marriage.

In 1908, Donlin almost single-handedly revivified the
stage as a place for ballplayers to make money in the off-
season. He took to the boards with Mabel in a baseball-
themed production called *Stealing Home.* In it, Donlin set
a new standard for that strange American hyphenate, the
athlete-actor. An adept base stealer on the ball field, he
proved he could shake a mean leg on the stage, too. The
New York World reported that Donlin's hoofing talents
"brought down the house." The *New York Globe* reported
that the dancing "created a small pandemonium of up-
roar." But *Variety*, the bible of show business, and cer-

tainly one of the most important reviews in town, positively gushed.

> If you haven't already attended the Big
> 42nd Street Ovation, by all means beg off
> from the office and do so without delay.
> Mike Donlin as a polite comedian is the
> most delightful vaudeville surprise you
> ever enjoyed, and if you miss him you do
> yourself an injustice.

They all liked Mabel, too.

If one were to wonder how Donlin could support two full-time careers simultaneously, the answer is very clear. He didn't. While many players would pick up good quick money with six-week appearances during the off-season, Donlin—much to John McGraw's fury—left baseball for the entire 1907, 1909, and 1910 seasons, all of which he dedicated to acting.

And he got away with it. Despite the occasional rumblings in the sporting press that he had "let his team down" (the Giants just missed pennants in all of these seasons), he remained a "popular idol," whose picture even appeared in *Vanity Fair* under the heading, "BROADWAY MIKE" DONLIN, THE BEAU BRUMMEL OF BASEBALL. Yet even his detractors conceded that Mike knew what he was doing: he was popularly believed to be making five times the amount of money in show business as McGraw had offered him to play for the Giants.

The success of the act of Hite & Donlin enabled them to collect a stratospheric $1,500 a week in New York and $2,000 a week on the road. "There is more money in being an actor than in being a ballplayer," Mike told an interviewer in 1909, a wonderfully perceptive statement that would resonate far into the future.

But Mike was right. It was simple economics. And the bottom ledger lines were not missed by other athletes, producers, and actresses. A marketable personality crossing over from sports to entertainment was big money, not just for the athlete but for anyone else in on the act. The principle would remain very clear in the short term on New York stages as well as for the rest of the century, even into the era of baseball free agency.

Lest the intertwining of baseball with show business be in any way underestimated, one other event toward the end of 1908 is well worth notation.

Consider the work of Jack Norworth and Albert Von Tilzer. Norworth was a composer and vaudeville performer. Von Tilzer was a lyricist. Together, they worked on Tin Pan Alley and turned out material for vaudeville with considerable success. "Considerable" might understate the point. Norworth performed with a female partner named Nora Bayes and the two were able to demand and get $1,750 per week on Broadway in 1907. Von Tilzer became a wealthy man by penning more than three thousand songs in his career.

Some Norworth-Von Tilzer concoctions were lasting. "I'll Be With You In Apple Blossom Time," for example.

Some were not. Who has recently heard of "Oh! How She Could Yacki, Hacki, Wicki, Wacki, Woo"?

But according to a story Norworth used to tell in subsequent years, the composer used to commute to work by train on a line that ran from Westchester County into Manhattan. Each day the train would pass the Polo Grounds.

Norworth had never been to a baseball game. But he had always wanted to go. And one morning his eyes settled upon one of Mr. McGraw's signs. It read,

BASEBALL TODAY — POLO GROUNDS

Norworth started playing with some lyrics and some sentiments. By the time he arrived at work, he had a set of lyrics, which he promptly turned over to Von Tilzer. A short time later, they had a popular song that would make them and their heirs a fortune over the ensuing decades.

Thus was conceived and written baseball's longtime anthem, "Take Me Out to The Ball Game."

4

◆

After winning two pennants during John McGraw's first five years as manager, the New York Giants suddenly fell into the position of a noble also-ran. They played winning baseball, but nonetheless were endlessly chasing the Cubs and the Pirates for the National League pennant. This brought no small anguish to John McGraw or John T. Brush. Thus by the end of 1908, when the Giants had again been skunked by the Chicago team—albeit by the narrowest of margins—McGraw was ready to put his team through a transition.

Rube Marquard, still only eighteen years old, was counted on to be part of the future. Other veterans such as "Iron Man" Joe McGinnity and Dummy Taylor were given their walking papers. Both McGinnity and Taylor were finished in major league baseball, though the "Iron Man," true to his nickname, pitched for an astonishing seventeen more years in the minors. In the two years after leaving the Giants, he pitched for Newark of the Eastern League, winning fifty-nine games in two seasons.

McGraw also swapped Roger Bresnahan to St. Louis

to satisfy Bresnahan's wish to manage. Bresnahan became the Cardinals' skipper on arrival. In return, McGraw picked up a solid outfielder, John "Red" Murray, and a pitcher named Arthur "Bugs" Raymond, who, had he not been a world-class alcoholic, might have been one of the best pitchers of his generation. The Cardinals were giving up on Raymond, who had been 14–25 for them in 1908. And already he was the brunt of many jokes around the league, most of them booze-related. Raymond was a spitballer, but one of the standard lines was that Bugs didn't lick the ball, he only exhaled on it. That way the ball would arrive at the plate drunk. McGraw naturally saw him as an ideal reclamation project.

Much of the atmosphere on the club was transitional also. There was a core of veterans like Mathewson, twenty-eight, Art Devlin, twenty-nine, and Red Ames, twenty-six who called the manager "Mac." Then there were the younger men such as Marquard, the youngest member of the club, now nineteen, Larry Doyle, twenty-two, and Fred Snodgrass, twenty-one, to whom the manager was — and would always be — "Mr. McGraw."

Sometimes this had nearly comic overtones.

Marquard was assigned to room with the great Mathewson at spring training and on the road, with no small reason being the hope that Mathewson's influence on the young lefty would be stellar, both personally and professionally. Mathewson and Marquard would chat about the manager to each other with the "Mr. McGraw" and "Mac" references sprinkled through the conversation, neither overstepping into the other's lexicon.

Spring training, too, was a transition, as McGraw and John Brush had selected in 1908 a little Texas town named Marlin Springs as their new training site.

Marlin was a sleepy little place, which hadn't changed much since the end of the Civil War. The town was so anxious to host the Giants that the city fathers deeded the town's ball park, Emerson Field, to the big club from New York for as many springs as the National Leaguers wanted to use it. Racially, Marlin Springs was as benighted a place as one might expect for central Texas in 1909, Marquard's first year in spring training.

One writer from New York filed an account of the Giants' players walking from their hotel to their practice field, "joshing" one another amiably "in the caressing morning sunlight . . . taking great draughts of the pure air, stopping at the Negro cabins to tease some mammy or take a snapshot of her pickaninny." At another time in capturing the atmosphere of Marlin, a writer for the *New York Times* reported that "a local white man" had "unloaded his artillery" at "three Negroes." Afterward, the *Times* reported, "the white man went on his way" while the "three colored gentlemen" were taken to the hospital.

Even the Polo Grounds had been spruced up that year. When the 1909 season started, players discovered that the grandstand had been painted a bright yellow, a move that opposing outfielders insisted had been designed to distract them from fly balls. Box seats had been suspended from the upper deck—an early concept of luxury boxes, one might argue—and the outfield had been enclosed by grandstands, raising the capacity of the horseshoe-shaped park to 30,000 seats. The only bigger sports facility in the U.S. was Harvard Stadium.

McGraw had high hopes for the season but found those hopes dashed very quickly. The loss of Donlin to vaudeville and Bresnahan to St. Louis were cited as main reasons that the Cubs and Pirates went out in front of New York early in the season and stayed there. But the loss of McGinnity and Taylor actually hurt, too. The pitchers whom McGraw expected to replace them (Ames, Raymond, and Marquard) simply weren't enough.

Ames won thirteen games, but lost ten. Raymond won eighteen games but served as such a huge distraction that he probably deflected much of McGraw's attention away from young Marquard. Raymond's record was deceptive, as he contributed less to the team than his numbers indicated. Yes, he was 18–12, but the wins were at the early part of the season. In between, he sabotaged the stability of the team with his frequent bouts of drunkenness. Once he engaged in a fistfight with McGraw on a train. At other times, McGraw fined Raymond for drinking, then secretly handed the money to Raymond's long-suffering wife.

"Great pitcher, Bugs is," McGraw told a sportswriter that year. "But a man can't drink thirty-five beers a day and stay in baseball." The thirty-five was apparently not an exaggeration.

McGraw tried everything to keep Raymond clean and sober. Once, particularly disgusted with Bugs, he left Raymond in a game when the pitcher was evidently drunk, and then let him suffer a ten-run inning at the hands of the Pirates. At another time, McGraw assigned a private detective to watch him. But Raymond was not just an alcoholic. He was also an ingenious alcoholic, sometimes stealing waiters' tip money in restaurants in order to buy himself a cheap bottle of booze.

One other time, devoid of money during the exhibition season in Texas, Bugs raided a waiters' setup room in which he found an entire table of cocktails. Within a minute or two, Bugs had knocked back six stiff drinks before a pair of waiters pried him loose from the table. On yet another occasion, when McGraw wouldn't allow him anything other than small change for Cokes and candies, Raymond devised the "magic shirt trick," wherein he could indulge in a serious binge by purchasing articles of clothing.

Here's how this ruse worked: Raymond asked for $12 (McGraw was by this time putting Bugs's paycheck directly into Mrs. Raymond's hands) to buy six shirts. Suspicious, McGraw sent along another player to the store with the twelve dollars. The shirts were purchased and Raymond showed them to McGraw.

McGraw nodded his approval, still suspicious.

Then Raymond went back to the store, returned the shirts for cash, took the twelve dollars, and tied on another drunk. On and on it went with Raymond until McGraw finally gave up and released him in 1911. Bugs never pitched again in the majors and despite the potential to be one of the best pitchers of his era, ended his career with a 44–54 record. Less than a year after his release from the Giants, Raymond — following a barroom brawl—drank himself to death in a Chicago hotel room at age thirty.

Had Raymond not served as such an utter distraction to McGraw, one wonders whether Marquard might have developed faster. Marquard's first full year in the National League was a disaster. He had great speed, a solid southpaw delivery, and a first-class curve ball. But the equation wasn't working, mainly because Marquard couldn't find the plate. His curve would break away from the strike zone and he would constantly fall behind on the count. He gave up an average of six or seven hits and four or five walks per game. The fans and the press, who had been anticipating immediate greatness considering the size of Rube's purchase price, turned against him quickly. The "$11,000 Beauty" soon was referred to in the press and the grandstands as the "$11,000 Lemon." Marquard had as much confidence as any young man entering the National League. But the battering he took in the newspapers and on the field went a long way to shake his confidence. When that happened, things only grew worse.

"Just go out there and pitch," McGraw told him repeatedly. "Don't listen to the fans, don't listen to the gamblers, don't listen to the writers. Just listen to *me*. Get out there and *pitch*."

Marquard never forgot the confidence shown by McGraw. Even though the two men would have their differences later in Marquard's Giant career, Marquard never had anything bad to say about his first major league skipper.

"What a great man he was," Marquard told Lawrence Ritter in 1966. "The finest and grandest man I ever met."

Yet, in 1909, Marquard was not getting it done. He was 6–13 for the season (in twenty-nine games) and was thoroughly unimpressive in most outings.

The next year, 1910, was a better one for the Giants.

The team was much more competitive, winning ninety-one games, and managing to hang in the pennant race—mathematically at least—for most of the season. There was also a pretty good spirit among spectators at the Polo Grounds. Broadway luminaries such as George M. Cohen, Lillian Russell, Will Rogers, Gentleman Jim Corbett, and DeWolf Hopper made nearly daily appearances at the park. Mayor James Gaynor, recovering from being shot in the head by a disgruntled city worker, was frequently in attendance. So was a newcomer, the world-renowned Gaelic tenor, John McCormick, who in packed concert halls in America's great cities, sang in a sweet voice of Irish lasses and the countryside of Erin—much to the misty-eyed delight of that Good Irishman, John McGraw.

Another Good Irishman, the indefatigable Mike Donlin, even offered to return to the club at midseason to see if he could help. McGraw and Brush, still sizzling over Donlin's "desertion" of the team on earlier occasions, rebuffed his offer.

But for Marquard, the season was even worse than 1909. New York finished in second place, thirteen games behind Chicago, and the absence of a big second starter (Mathewson had won twenty-seven games again) was the club's most glaring deficiency. The Giants were missing, in other words, the pitcher that Marquard had been intended to be. To make matters worse, Rube was dropped to the seventh position on the pitching staff and soon found himself in a mop-up role in the bull pen. It was difficult to figure which was worse for Rube, coming into games in the late innings, or sitting in the bull pen, close to the fans, listening to their daily excoriations of him. Like New York fans of any other era, there was nothing subtle about the riding they gave him.

McGraw, hoping to somehow catch the Cubs, managed to give Marquard only eight starts all year (of a total of a meager thirteen appearances) and only two starts turned into quality performances.

Rube's final statistics of 4–4 with a 4.46 ERA were not the numbers that the fans and writers in New York had expected from such a highly touted rookie. Not even Marquard's roommate Christy Mathewson could understand what had happened to the most promising prospect ever signed by the Giants.

"I had an awful time," Marquard said more than fifty years later, thinking back to those first two full seasons in the big town. "The New York papers gave me a great sendoff, but they really overdid it. They set a standard I could never live up to, and it began two years of bitter disappointment for me. It still makes me uncomfortable when I think about it."

It is safe to say that the seasons of 1909 and 1910, Rube's first two in New York, were both personally and professionally the unhappiest two summers of his life.

When the regular season of 1910 ended, the Philadelphia A's defeated the Chicago Cubs in a five-game World Series. New York fans still had a chance to see the local heroes, however.

A city series was proposed between the Giants and the New York American League team, then known as the Highlanders. The latter had surprised many people in baseball by finishing second to Connie Mack's Philadelphia A's. The New York Americans were led by the ever-villainous remorselessly venal Hal Chase, whose talent as a first baseman was surpassed only by his skill in sabotaging managers and tanking ball games. The Highlanders also featured a pair of wily spitballers named Russ Ford (26–6) and John Pincus Quinn (18–12).

The ascendance of the Highlanders was not necessarily a wonderful development for McGraw. He dared not look as if he were avoiding the series, and he dared not lose it either. So after conferring with team owner John Brush, McGraw accepted the challenge. The matchup would be sort of a shadow World Series, best four out of seven for the purported championship of Upper Manhattan.

Accepting the challenge was a wise decision. The Giants won the series 4–1, with a sixth game ending in a tie. Bragging rights for America's number-one sports town remained with the National League club and McGraw managed to rehearse his strategy for the following season: his Giants stole successfully nineteen times in the six games. Rookie Josh Devore, a quick-as-mercury base runner whom McGraw was now ready to turn loose in the National League, personally managed six thefts.

Mathewson, however, was the star of the series, winning three complete games and saving the fourth. He walked one batter in thirty innings and managed all this after a season in which he had already pitched 319 innings and been 27–9. The parallels with the 1905 World Series, in which the great Matty had pitched three shutouts in three starts, were all over New York's sports pages.

There was also a nice financial payoff for the Giants' players. Paid attendance for the six games had exceeded 110,000. Each Giant took home $1,100. Each Highlander pocketed $706. No player complained that the season should have been shorter.

Mathewson, along with his catcher, Chief Meyers, then had the occasion to pick up some more money and present himself to the public once again. Sportswriter Bozeman Bugler wrote a skit for the two titled *Curves*, and wisely included a part for a perky actress named May Tully. Following the success of Mike Donlin and Mabel Hite a few years earlier, the skit played successfully on Broadway for seventeen weeks. Mathewson reportedly received a nifty $1,000 per week.

Nor were Mathewson and Meyers alone on stage that autumn. On a lesser scale in Philadelphia, Phillies' catcher Red Dooin performed songs and even had a speaking role with a famous Philly group called Dumont's Minstrels. And in Chicago, a White Sox pitcher named Doc White capped a 15–13 season by composing the music

for a ballad titled "Little Puff of Smoke, Good Night."
The suspiciously suggestive lyrics were by that noted sub-
versive, Ring Lardner. And even the great but mean-spirited Ty Cobb—who in later years would insist that he
had spent off-seasons vigorously keeping in shape—took
the occasion to star in a durable stage comedy called *The
College Widow.* The show toured New York, Chicago and
Detroit and Cobb did not receive bad notices.

It was becoming clearer with each passing season that
there was big-time dough in show business for any athlete clever enough and prominent enough—though not
necessarily *talented* enough—to cash in.

5

$\blacklozenge$

By the end of 1910 there were hundreds of stages—vaudeville, legitimate, and burlesque—in New York and thousands in smaller circuits across the U.S. Competition was fierce among the thousands of actors vying for the chance to make either a living or a fortune.

Critics were both important and influential and the daily reviewers in particular had a significant amount of clout. There was, after all, no television, no radio, and no coverage by weekly magazines. How could one decide where to spend one's silver entertainment dime unless one read in the daily press what was good and, conversely, what was not so good? Certain theater chains had their "friendlies" who always gave their shows a good review. Louis De Foe of the *New York Morning World* and Charles Darton of the *New York Evening World* displayed a remarkable propensity for Shubert shows, which in turn caused the Shuberts to drop many advertising dollars in the two editions of the *World*. Make of it what you will, but De Foe and Darton were *so* dependable that the Shuberts left the two critics' names in lights in the electric sign over the Winter Garden Theater. The Shuberts displayed enormous confidence that any show they opened would get a good quote, at the very least, from the *World*. More than one Broadway cynic privately wondered just how many payrolls De Foe and Darton were on.

De Foe and Darton notwithstanding, many reviewers in New York became masters of the verbal stiletto. When producer Willie Hammerstein presented a ballet titled *Marguerite* at his Olympic Theater, it included a circus number with four young women dancing under the guidance of the ringmaster.

Wrote Alan Dale in the *New York Journal*,

> If those horses had tails, I could have written a great story.

In reviewing Otero, a small, shrill-voiced Spanish dancer, Acton Davies of the *New York Sun* wrote,

> We have seen Otero sing. We have heard her dance.

In revealing his thoughts on a play about the Spanish-American War, the play having just opened at the Grand Opera House in Manhattan, Davies's tongue was just as sharp.

> The second act of the play takes place in a castle, which, like most of the women in the play, had been ruined by the Spaniards.

And then there was Heywood Broun, who wrote for the *New York Tribune* and who—when properly provoked—could rise to an eloquent savagery equal to none. Broun, who later became a pretty good monologist himself on stage, once ripped into Mlle Eva Tanguay, the highly successful and highly popular French chanteuse.

Wrote Monsieur Broun,

> Miss Tanguay sings in French and I have no idea if she is trying to be funny. I never know what she is trying to be except noisy. I think she is the parsnip of performers. The only cheerful song in her repertoire yesterday was one in which she hinted that she might soon retire. Miss Tanguay is billed as a "bombshell." Would be to Heaven that she were, for a bomb is something that is taken to a great height and then dropped.

Among the most important reviews were those in *Variety*, as that paper, in addition to a candid opinion of an actor or a production, would also note whether or not the audience laughed, what the paid admission was, and other details important to producers and booking agents. It is also true that *Variety*'s impact was chiefly upon vaudeville and burlesque houses for exactly those reasons. Legitimate theater audiences tended to read a review or two and, unless the review was a rave or a slam, make up their own mind.

Epes Winthrop Sargent, who reviewed for *Variety* for many years under the byline of Chicot, provided an insight into not just the bluntness of some of his reviews, but also the bloodthirsty tone of many reviews in general.

> The average actor was too dumb to appreciate the niceties of language,

chirped "Chicot."

> I could not say (someone) was a bad actor. I had to tell him he was a damned bad actor. . . . It was taking a chance telling an acrobat that his comedy would make a horse vomit, but it was part of the risk and I only got one black eye.

Not that the actors couldn't sling it back. They could, with equal venom. One actor, getting on a train, once remarked to a rural critic who had given him a bad write-up, "When that whistle toots, I'll be outside your circulation." Another thespian once cracked, "A reviewer is a guy whose parents wanted a boy." Still another suggested that, "A critic is a newspaperman whose sweetheart ran away with an actor."

And then there was the ultimate slam by actors upon those who reviewed them, a comment attributed to many but probably as old as the jousting between show people and those who wrote about them.

"I don't mind you panning my act," the line went, "because today's newspaper is the toilet paper of tomorrow."

One actor who received his share of favorable onstage notices over a long career was Joe Kane.

Joe Kane was born in Pittsburgh in 1883 and at birth bore the name of either Joseph Cahane or Joseph Cohen, depending on which edition of his birth certificate one checks. He spent the early part of his boyhood in the smoky city, and in later years maintained that he had been drawn to the stage from as far back as he could remember. At the age of eleven, however, pushed into the horse racing business by his parents, he became a jockey, riding at a handful of tracks in the West and Midwest.

His career on horseback ended four years later, when he grew too big to ride. But the stage had always been his first love, and even as a boy hanging around the nags, he would entertain the backstretch crew with songs and dances. There is no surviving word on how well his performances were appreciated, but a hanger-on whom he met in the stables did see something in the young man and talked Kane into going on the road with a traveling side show. So at age fifteen, Joe toured the country for forty weeks, singing, dancing, and serving as the barker out front until the show skipped town. Not long afterward, he graduated to eastern vaudeville, doing a formidable schedule of nine-a-day shows at a salary of $15 a week for himself and his partner. This was a typical turn-of-the-century apprenticeship in show biz and, as such, it was brutal. But a would-be performer either learned his craft or quickly washed out of the business.

Joe learned his craft, and while one might have questioned how far Kane's ability would take him, the determination and dedication were always there. In many ways, he typified the American spirit of the early part of this century.

"I have great faith in the belief that when a person sets out to do a certain thing and thinks about it constantly, it is possible to accomplish it, though it may be very difficult to do," Kane once told a reporter years after he had become a regular player on Broadway.

"I've known some four or five of my acquaintances," Kane went on, "boys about my own age who had made up their minds that they were going to do certain things when they became men. All of them have met with success. Two became lawyers, one a physician, one is a dentist, and the other an engineer. I was bent on becoming an actor. As a boy, I was always talking about going onstage. In fact, I couldn't talk much upon other subjects. When in my room alone, I would practice before a mirror. I am proud of the fact that I have not failed in my youthful ambition."

In the heyday of vaudeville, a staple of many shows was the "single woman" act. This was not what one might immediately suspect. The "single woman" acts were, as vaudevillian Joe Laurie, Jr. described them in *Vaudeville:*

From the Honky Tonks to The Palace, "the gals who used to belt over any kind of song—comedy, ballad, or novelty. And I mean belt them over on their own power without the aid of an engineer, P.A. system, microphone (or) fancy arrangements." Among the most famous were Fanny Brice, Molly Picon, Helen Morgan, Sophie Tucker, Eva (Heywood Broun's favorite) Tanguay, and Bonnie Thornton.

Thornton, however, also appeared with her husband, James J. Thornton, who was a wit and monologist. Unfortunately, James J. Thornton was also one of the most legendary drunks of his era, his sparkling wit and hilarious monologues sometimes lost in a tidal wave of booze. Once Bonnie locked James in their hotel room to keep him sober for a performance. James beat this scenario by having a bellboy line up a pint of liquor and a straw through the keyhole of the hotel room.

How does this circle back to Joe Kane? When Kane was a younger man, Thornton, for reasons bibulous, was sometimes unable to go on. So Kane worked an act with Bonnie Thornton—no small accomplishment, as Bonnie was a significant star already—in which Kane would sing to her from the theater balcony. And she would sing back.

Bonnie, a well-liked, long-suffering woman known on stage as "the little magnet," generally drew favorable press notices in New York as well as good audiences. When Kane performed with her, he was noticed in the big city. This was around 1903. Joe was barely twenty.

Many of the star attractions in early vaudeville were two-person acts, such as Smith & Dale, Bayes & Norworth, and Burns & Allen. These teams put on short skits or even full-length productions that highlighted the principals, but that also needed a few supporting actors. One such team, Mathews and Bulger, hired Joe Kane to play a supporting role in a show titled, *At Gay Coney Island*. Kane played "a dude," according to the credits. One must recall that the title of the piece, as well as Kane's role, meant something different in the terminology of the day.

Other productions followed quickly. Kane came under the able management of one George W. Lederer and, in the first years of the twentieth century, Joe earned excellent notices in a number of big Broadway productions, not the least of which was George M. Cohan's original *Yankee Doodle Dandy*. Also highly noteworthy was Kane's performance as — of all things — an insane man in a production titled *The Belle of New York*.

Kane also became known as a "Dutch comedian." This type of act was not exactly subtle and played heavily upon the previously discussed prejudices of the time, mimicking German accents and attitudes, often with little substance to the act other than crude ethnic parody.

But Kane's *ability* as a "Dutchman" lent him a certain popularity, even among Germans in the audience. Eventually, in 1906 he worked as a supporting player in shows performed by a "Dutch" comedy team named The Rogers Brothers. Kane was gifted enough to also understudy both main roles — played by Gus Rogers and Max Rogers — while remaining a supporting player in the cast.

The humor, such as it was, of Gus and Max was broad,

to put it gently. Much of it evolved from the portrayal of a couple of buffoonish Germans in preposterous situations and equally preposterous attire. Rambling through an improbable foreign country was considered a source of endless mirth, as was dressing up in ridiculous Mitteleuropa *Wo-Is-Der-Hauptbahnhof?* outfits, complete with epaulets, gaudy rope belts and hats left over from the Franco-Prussian war.

Here is an example of a typical "Double Dutch" act of the day.

A straightman and comedian come on stage. The straight man wears a garish plaid suit, the comedian wears a belly pad to make him look shorter and fatter than he is. They both wear fake beards and sing a few bars of a popular song. Abruptly, the harmony ends and the orchestra plays a note of discord.

Then the exchange begins.

BOTH
(shaking hands)
By golly. Dot vos all right!

STRAIGHT MAN
Hey, Fritz! I hear your uncle vot
ain't dead yet left you a lot of money.

COMEDIAN
(shows big roll of dollar bills)
Zure. Here 'tis.

STRAIGHT MAN
Vot you going to do mit it?

COMEDIAN
Don't know. I dink I'll zell it to
zomebody.

And so it went.

Soon other events conspired to boost Kane's career.

In 1906, Max Rogers took ill. Kane immediately stepped into the starring role in a production titled *The Rogers Brothers in Ireland*. Then in mid-1908, Gus Rogers took ill while performing that year's edition of the team's kraut-bashing travelogue, *The Rogers Brothers in Panama*. Shortly thereafter, Gus died. And yet, even then the show had to go on. Kane became a Broadway star handling the late actor's role, with considerable support from the late comedian's friends and with excellent write-ups in the New York press.

> Mr. Kane bears a striking resemblance, both as to looks and manners, to the late Gus Rogers,

wrote the *New York Telegraph* in October of 1908.

> When (Kane) was playing the part when Gus Rogers was ill, few of Mr. Rogers's closest friends knew that it was Joseph Kane . . . doing the acting.

Indeed. Twice in three seasons Kane had saved a Rogers production by stepping in for one of the stars. Such things were never lost on Broadway insiders. Thus, upon Gus Rogers's untimely death, Joe Kane climbed another rung on the Broadway and vaudeville ladder. He wasn't the biggest star in town, but he was no longer an understudy, either.

At the same time, Blossom Seeley was climbing toward stardom at the two-a-day shows in Los Angeles and Rube Marquard, eighteen years old, was on his way back to Ohio for the winter, his first game in the National League having proven a disaster. But it was also at about this time that events began to put all three on a collision course.

In early 1909, a touring production of *In Panama* traveled the country — the title had been shortened since there was now only one live Rogers Brother. Eventually, the show closed. Kane, having built a reasonable following on the legit stage with The Rogers Brothers, returned to New York vaudeville in November of 1909, opening a fourteen-minute act called *A Bunch of Foolishness.*

Kane was supported by four actresses who went only under the name of "Some Girls." The act played the recently opened Greenpoint Theater in Brooklyn. Kane appeared early on the bill and despite weak material — Joe was still working his Dutchman shtick — the act played well.

"Kane works hard, keeping things lively throughout," *Variety* reported. The new act kept Joe working into 1910.

During the following spring, however, Joe Kane went

back out west to tour with another show. Working a theater in Chicago he came upon a singer-actress of whom
he had heard, but never met. It was Blossom Seeley. She
was just coming off a hugely successful thirty-eight-week
stand in Los Angeles and was working her act through
Chicago, Milwaukee, and smaller cities in between.

Joe was both immediately smitten and persuasive.
With her assent he had an act devised that opened successfully in Milwaukee: Blossom Seeley & Joe Kane. A
name from the West and a name from the East. But even
Joe could see who the more talented half of their partnership was.

"Blossom will prove to be one of the most popular
young women ever to play vaudeville," Joe told friends.

The prediction would prove to carry pinpoint accu-
racy for many years. And very quickly, Kane made an
abrupt career change.

JOE KANE RETIRES

ran an astonishing headline in the *New York Review*, on
September 24, 1910.

Then the article continued.

> Joe Kane conveys the impression that he
> has given up acting as a means of liveli-
> hood, which is rather a pity. . . . However,
> Mr. Kane has been working out west with
> a girl team mate named Blossom Seeley,
> for whom the big vaudeville circuits pro-

duce a string of contracts running far into the future and calling for terms quite fabulous. . . . Hereupon, Mr. Kane will pause in his own artistic career to devote himself to promoting that of Miss Seeley, whose business manager he has become. All the same, it is too bad to lose him.

But New York audiences were at little risk of "losing" Joe. Kane had actually just put himself in the position to take the role in life for which he would be best remembered. For Joe not only took over as Blossom's business manager, the early equivalent of a theatrical agent, but also began to court her as well.

Growing up in San Francisco, having been on stage as a young girl, and being by all accounts considered quite pretty by the standards of the day — with a tendency to be a little plump, which didn't hurt back then, either — Blossom was no stranger to the advances of attractive older men. Whether Joe came on as a slick Broadway guy — albeit via Pittsburgh — or just an experienced older man who knew his way around show business is open to question. There were probably elements of both in his approach to Blossom and the trust she gave him. Nonetheless, Kane and Seeley were quickly an item in New York.

Which made things all the more convenient for Joe.

Kane was in the position of bringing a hot out-of-town property — Blossom — to Broadway. Kane had experience and plenty of contacts in show business. They paid off quickly.

Kane landed Seeley a role in a production called *The Hen-Pecks*, a big twenty-three character musical comedy extravaganza that had previously played out of town. In January 1911, the Broadway Theater closed down for three weeks so that carpenters and technicians could get the stage ready for the rehearsals of the massive performing company. Lew Fields, Seeley's mentor from Los Angeles, starred in the show. Kane landed a role for himself as a character with the unlikely name of "Ravioli." And Blossom played a character with the even less likely name of Henella Peck.

This is not the type of production you would catch in the current day. The show was a group of loosely connected skits, most of them using a barnyard motif. The opening curtain, for example, rose on "a real barnyard," featuring "chickens, ducks, geese, and a young pig." But other scenes were set in places as disparate as a barber shop, Times Square, and a lunch counter in a railroad station, the animals presumably back in the wings during these dramatic endeavors. And there were cast members who were present simply to showcase their talents for a scene or two, such as a man named Frank Whitman, who did a dance to the accompaniment of his own violin playing.

The story, such as it was, surrounded a henpecked husband played by Lew Fields. His character was named—surprise and guffaw!—Henry Peck. In case the audience still didn't get the joke, or didn't want the joke to end, there were various women characters named Heniola Peck, Henriette Peck, and Henoria Peck. Other roles, and this apparently really set the audience to cluckling, were named Weenie Wistaria, Pansy Marsh-mallow, and Mlle Twinkle Toes. There was also a character named Major Manley. The humor here was not what you might expect, as Major Manley was portrayed by an actress named Hazel Allen.

Back to Blossom, however, who played Henella Peck. This was Blossom's usual "soubrette" role, packaged neatly again, but for the first time on Broadway. She had a song to sing, something new to present to a fresh audience and it was a number imported from out west called "Toddling The Todalo."

Opening night came on February tenth. And Blossom brought down the house with her performance.

"The Hen-Pecks is the biggest most satisfying entertainment to arrive here in years!" proclaimed *Variety*, in pronouncing the show a hit. Several cast members were cited as outstanding, but even among them, Seeley was singled out.

Blossom was "wonderful," according to *Variety*. And "her song and dance in the second act established her as a future local favorite!"

Her song and dance? Blossom had something that, in addition to herself, caught everyone's attention.

"Ever hear of 'The Bunny Hug'?" breathlessly enthused the *New York Review*. "No? Then see 'The Todalo!'"

Follow this closely. The Todalo, the press agents for the show explained, was a West Coast variation of The Turkey Trot, which itself was an imitation of the strutting of a turkey just before Thanksgiving. The Todalo,

the newspapers of the day went on to explained, origi-
nated on the "Barbary Coast" of San Francisco, where it
was known not as The Todalo or The Turkey Trot but
rather as The Bunny Hug, though the San Francisco version of The Bunny Hug was actually a refined version of
the same, which is why, presumably, its name was
changed to The Todalo.

Okay so far?

Then next consider that "The Todalo" was a South-
west and West Coast slang word for the "tenderloin" section of a city, that is, the section noted for vice, corruption, and "sinful" entertainment, and so-named tenderloin because the police taking bribes there could live so
well on the proceeds of local corruption.

But the real significance of the performance was that
Blossom had hoofed into New York with a new two step
and knocked audiences dead. Her cameo performances —
one in each act of *The Hen-Pecks* – stopped the show. The
music was sharply syncopated, finger-snapping ragtime,
something that would become a Seeley trademark over
the ensuing years. And remember that Seeley was coming into town from San Francisco, that den of iniquity in
the West. Just knowing that lent an extra pizzazz to the
performance.

Remember, too, those vampirish critics who seemed
to dine on the blood of performers? Seeley turned them
into purring pussy cats.

> They say that only a native California can
> dance The Todalo in its true spirit,

wrote one reviewer.

> It is certain that nobody could put more
> fire and vim into it than Miss Seeley, who
> was born in San Francisco . . . . The com-
> bined success of artist and performance has
> been such that it will be a long time before
> The Todalo will be allowed to toddle off to
> its native haunts.

Or, more succinctly,

> Blossom Seeley is excellent!

wrote the *New York American*.

> Go see her!

And so that quickly, under the management and romantic eye of Joe Kane, Seeley was a star in New York. It
was February 1911, and Blossom was settling in for a long
stay in big-time show business.

In the spring, Seeley left *The Hen-Pecks*, switched from
the legit stage back to vaudeville for a brief New York
run, then joined the great Al Jolson—who had evolved
from blackface by now—for a national tour of *The Whirl
of Society*. By the summer, she was not just a West Coast
star or a New York star.

She was a *national* star with emerging sex appeal.

By her own arithmetic, she was just twenty years old.

And at twenty, she was just one year younger than Rube Marquard, who in that same year, was facing make-or-break time with the New York Giants.

6

In March 1911, John McGraw returned the New York Giants to Marlin Springs, Texas, for the fourth spring training in a row.

The men who comprised the Giants were by now familiar figures—for better or worse—to the residents of the little prairie town one hundred miles south of Dallas.

McGraw had chosen Marlin Springs because it was "out of the way." No one ever took issue with that. McGraw's subtext was clear, also. He would have more control over his players if he could supervise them in a small, enclosed environment where, presumably, everyone knew everyone else's business.

John Kieran, writing in the *New York Times* during the first decade of this century, once described contemporary spring training sites as an unending series of episodes of athletes goofing off, playing crude practical jokes on one another, and getting into playing shape at their own pace.

"The camps," Kieran wrote, "are crowded with ducks left swimming in bathtubs, young alligators tucked under the pillows of unsuspecting sleepers, and snipe hunts all night long in the hills with starry-eyed rookies left holding the bag." There was, of course, a darker side to some of the players' antics in springtime, one which rarely found its way into print. Suffice it to say that local men with wives and daughters were not keen on having a bunch of rowdy athletes in town, separated from their regular girlfriends or spouses, with too much time on their hands.

McGraw attempted to redefine spring training in this era by watching his players carefully and working them hard. Once at the training camp, McGraw ran as tough a ship as any manager in either league. Players were required to walk the half-mile distance from the Arlington Hotel to the training site, and back, for example. But this didn't mean there wasn't time for some socialization. Fish fries, benefit intrasquad games for local charities, and an annual community dance were parts of every spring in Marlin. McGraw personally contributed to the local economy with losses at poker with the town's best players, losses he sometimes recouped at bridge, wisely using the cerebral Mathewson as his partner. McGraw was also in the habit of making late-night visits to certain back-alley saloons where black musicians played enthusiastic ragtime music.

And then there were the times when local feathers got ruffled and McGraw had to soothe them. Larry Doyle had the hilarious — or so he thought — habit of throwing firecrackers under the chair of any sportswriter he caught dozing in the hotel lobby. In a more serious incident,

Marquard once decided that it would be great fun to fire a pistol out the hotel window. This may have been Texas, where gun ownership has always been close to religion, but the Marlin police chief didn't let that issue drop until McGraw threatened to pull his team out of town.

Nonetheless, spring training of 1911 went as smoothly as could be hoped. And this year above all, McGraw had plans for Marquard.

Young Rube had just turned twenty-one the previous October and McGraw felt, with reason, that the moment was at hand for the young fireballer to graduate to becoming a major league hurler. He was 9–18 in forty-three major league appearances so far and it was time to make things happen. McGraw was tired of hearing that he had wasted his money on the kid from Cleveland, a notion that the New York sportswriters had been suggesting for two years now. No one was more anxious to get what he had paid for than McGraw. The manager was hardly unaware that five seasons had passed since he had last won a pennant. And even fresher in his mind was the fact that the Giants had finished second in 1910, a whopping 13 1/2 games behind the Cubs. The Cubs had won four of the last five National League pennants (Pittsburgh won the other in 1909) and had twice won the World Championship. Changes were in order; improvements had to be made. McGraw, a man who abhorred losing, could not have been an entirely happy man in early 1911. But as always, McGraw had a plan.

Years previously, when McGraw had been the third baseman for the Orioles, the regular catcher had been a stocky catcher named Wilbert Robinson. Robinson had great baseball sense, particularly when it came to handling pitchers.

As a kid in Massachusetts, Robinson hadn't bothered much with formal education—as would become apparent in later years—occupying himself instead by driving a horse-drawn fishmonger's wagon and earning the nickname of Billy Fish. In baseball lore, particularly as he grew older, wider, and more avuncular, he would be known as Uncle Robbie. Or sometimes Uncle Wilbie. Author Robert Creamer once described Robinson as "a pleasantly profane fatman," which just about hit the nail perfectly on the head. Some would also uncharitably refer to Robinson as "slow-witted," which would not have exactly been inaccurate, either.

There are many stories about Robinson when he eventually became manager of the Brooklyn Dodgers in 1914. The Dodgers, incidentally, were renamed the "Robins" in his honor during his tenure. There was the time when Uncle Robbie wanted to start Oscar Roettger at first base instead of Claude Hendricks. When he couldn't spell Roettger's name on the lineup card, however, Robinson rethought his decision and started Hendricks. At another time, Brooklyn catcher Zack Taylor tripled to start the ninth inning in a game in which Brooklyn trailed by a run. Robinson, coaching third, beamed with pride.

"Put 'er there!" he exclaimed, extending his hand from the coaching box.

When Taylor did as he was told, stepping off the base to extend his hand, he was tagged out.

And then there was the time that Robinson finally grew tired of his players making "bonehead" plays. So the day came when he started "The Bonehead Club," an early baseball version of the locker room kangaroo court. Anyone on the team doing something really dumb — and there was no shortage of such incidents — would be fined ten dollars. A few minutes later, Robinson handed that day's umpires the previous day's lineup card, creating a batting-out-of-order situation that cost Brooklyn the game. He paid the ten dollars.

In his youth, however, Robinson had been a pretty decent player — a man with good physical skills and a surprisingly good grasp of the game, even if he was un-lettered and often inarticulate. In June 1892, while catch-ing with the Orioles, Robinson whacked out seven hits in seven at-bats in one game, driving in eleven runs in the process. The RBI record stood for many years. The hits-in-a-game record stands today — though it remained unknown until 1912, when Robinson casually mentioned the game to Harvard-educated reporter Heywood Broun, who covered both baseball and Broadway for the *New York Herald*.

Robinson became one of John McGraw's closest friends when the two were with the Orioles. They opened a cafe and bowling establishment named The Diamond where the game of duckpins was invented. The beanery business thrived, but the partners sold out when McGraw moved to New York in 1902.

Robinson stayed behind in Baltimore as player man-ager, but not for long. Robinson had had one finger amputated in 1896. When another one became injured in 1904, he could no longer play the game. So he retired and opened a butcher shop, bringing to the business many of the skills he had displayed so ably on the baseball field. Once years later, for example, when the Dodgers were in Chicago, Robinson took his players on a tour of the stockyards. On the invitation from a meat packer, Uncle Robbie picked up an executioner's hammer and killed a steer with one well-aimed blow to the head.

The butcher business was exactly where Robinson was in the off-season of 1910–11 when McGraw contacted him and asked him to come to the Giants as a pitching coach. His pet project was to be Rube Marquard. Robinson, who had been following the faltering career of the Giants' prized young hurler, accepted the assignment.

They must have made a strange-looking duo that spring, Robinson and Marquard, a Mutt and Jeff of the Texas prairie. Robinson stood five feet eight with two hundred twenty pounds hanging on his round frame. He was graying and showed the ravages of having caught 1,316 National League games, many of them before the days of shin guards and a catcher's mask. Rube, of course, was seven inches taller and forty to fifty pounds lighter and approaching the peak of his handsome-young-athlete looks. Upon his arrival in Texas, Robinson quickly went to work with Rube, studying him for a few days, then starting to make suggestions.

"Robbie devoted himself almost entirely to Marquard in the spring of 1911," Christy Mathewson later recalled.

"He used to take Rube into some corner every day and talk to him for hours. This was the time when the papers were calling (Rube) the $11,000 Lemon and urging McGraw to let Marquard go in exchange for some capable batboy. . . . Out there in the hot Texas sun, Robinson gave Rube the confidence he had lacked."

Robinson also dropped an earlier experiment that had been McGraw's idea, which was getting Marquard to throw overhand more than sidearm. Some observers had contended that McGraw's tampering with young Marquard's delivery was a cause of the latter's delay in developing. Uncle Robbie also gave his pupil some thorough lessons about the philosophy of the game. Robinson showed Marquard two flaws in his mental approach to pitching: Often Rube would get two quick strikes on a batter, then let up until he got himself in a hole. Other times, Marquard wouldn't go directly after a batter fast enough and would find himself behind in the count immediately. These at-bats often resulted in either walks (when Marquard couldn't find the plate) or hits (when he found too much of the plate). Robinson sought to remedy these habits by teaching Rube to throw a first-pitch strike, then mixing his locations and alternating fastballs and curves.

It could also be argued that Robinson taught the young left-hander a new pitch, convincing him to throw a sharply breaking curve instead of the old sweeping roundhouse curve that had worked earlier in Marquard's career. The roundhouse had been good enough to retire batters in the American Association, Robinson pointed out. But, to state the obvious, the National League was not the American Association.

Rube, thinking back to the bitter disappointments of his first two full seasons with the Giants, was not in a position to argue. So he listened to Robinson and heeded his advice. In the spring, Rube looked sharp. Robinson and McGraw — and for that matter Rube — had reason to be optimistic when the team broke camp in April and headed north, stopping to play exhibitions from Texas to Baltimore, before arriving in New York to open the season.

Opening day in New York was April 13 and the Philadelphia Phillies provided the opposition. The date was an event.

Close to 30,000 fans — or "bugs" as they were sometimes still called — crowded into the ballpark to see the game. The stadium was decorated with red, white, and blue bunting. The grassy playing surface was in excellent condition, thanks to the painstaking efforts of John Murphy, the head groundskeeper. In keeping with the Hibernian links that the club would always have during its tenure in New York, Murphy had also planted small Irish flags — emerald green with the gold harp — at second base and in right field, where those most Gaelic of Irish stars, Larry Doyle and Red Murray, would open the season. Needless to say, a good Irishman like McGraw had no problem with the tiny green flags.

In the choice box seats near the Giants' dugout, John McGraw's pals from the entertainment world were well represented. Delegations from both the Lambs' and the Friars' clubs were there, including George M. Cohan, the veteran showman, DeWolf Hopper, who made a career out of reciting *Casey At The Bat* across America, and Eddie Foy, one of the biggest vaudeville entertainers of the day. A brass band cranked out a rousing version of "East Side, West Side" in honor of the home nine and McGraw accepted a huge floral horseshoe from club management, a good luck charm — it was hoped — for the nascent season.

Then the game began. Ever with an eye toward attendance, McGraw started Red Ames, holding Mathewson back until Saturday in order to draw another big crowd on the weekend. Ames pitched well, but Earl Moore of the Phillies pitched better, and the Giants lost 2–0.

And thus a memorable season was underway. Not all the memories, however, would be pleasant.

Just after midnight following opening day, a night watchman near the elevated train tracks adjacent to the Polo Grounds saw flames in the vicinity of the ballpark. Looking more closely, the watchman realized the flames were *in* the park and shooting up from the wooden grandstands. New York's number-one sports building was on fire.

The blaze had started in the right centerfield bleachers, probably as a result of a discarded cigar or cigarette. Once the blaze was underway, however, it developed into one of the most spectacular conflagrations of its time. Horse-drawn firefighting equipment responded in the middle of the night, but little could be saved other than a section of outfield bleachers. So here the Giants were in April 1911, anxious to defend their championship. Now, in the second day of the season, they had lost their home opener as well as their home.

The most immediate question the team faced was where to play. A solution came from an unexpected source. After feuding with McGraw and Giant management for years, Frank Farrell, owner of the New York Highlanders in the American League, invited the Giants to move temporarily into Hilltop Park. John Brush, the Giants owner, accepted immediately.

Hilltop Park stood atop Morningside Heights at Broadway between 165th and 168th streets. (Today, Columbia-Presbyterian Medical Center stands on the real estate that Hilltop Park occupied. There is no marker whatsoever commemorating what was the birthplace of the New York Yankees.) The name Hilltop was logical, as the park was at the highest point in Manhattan—hence the designation of "the Highlanders" for the club that played there. Hilltop Park was a rickety wooden structure that was already outmoded by 1911. It belonged to the generation of ballparks that was hastily constructed at the turn of the century, built for cheapness and quickness, with the thought of herding in as many people as often as possible. Like the old Polo Grounds, it was a top-of-the-line firetrap, and the wonder was—since smoking was more common than not among its frequently drunken patrons—that it, too, never burned to the ground. And, strangely enough, the two most noteworthy incidents that ever occurred in the park both involved Ty Cobb.

First, in 1909, a photographer named Charles Conlon snapped a picture of Cobb sliding into third base, his spikes kicking up a hailstorm of dirt, his face clenched in aggression and anger, as New York third baseman Jimmy Austin took a late throw from the outfield. The shot became one of baseball's most famous pictures. Then, three years later, Cobb charged into the Hilltop stands to pummel a crippled fan who had called him a "half-nigger." The incident caused Cobb to be suspended and his teammates to "strike" in sympathy. The next day amateur ballplayers donned Tiger uniforms to lose in Philadelphia, 24–2.

At the time of the 1911 fire at the Polo Grounds, Brush's health was failing. A victim of locomotor ataxia, a disorder of the nervous system, Brush was frail and practically an invalid. Nonetheless, the Giants owner visited the ruins of his ballpark the day after the fire, pushed in his wheelchair across the playing field by his wife, Elsie. Brush made a bold decision. He had been impressed with the new concrete and steel baseball stadiums that two other major league franchises had recently erected. The Shibe family had built a new park for the Athletics in Philadelphia in 1908 and had named it after themselves. Barney Dreyfus, owner of the Pittsburgh Club, built a similar stadium in the Smoky City and named it after a Revolutionary war general, John Forbes.

Brush, in the last two years of his life, now had a similar vision.

"Elsie," he said as he toured the smoldering ruins of his park, "I want to build a concrete stand. The finest that can be constructed. It will mean economy for a while. Will you stand with me?" What else could Elsie say, particularly with the press in close attendance?

The team moved temporarily to Hilltop. Brush's architects went to work on plans the next day. By May, the team was ready to call a press conference at the fashionable Claremont Inn, right across the street from Grant's Tomb, to unveil the plans for what was described in the hyperbole of the day as the Eighth Wonder of the World.

It was something short of the Pyramids along the Nile, but it *was* a new concrete and steel structure for baseball. The initial plans envisioned an eventual forty-five thousand seats (over the years, the capacity was expanded to fifty-five thousand with upper decks and grandstands) and it would be constructed where the ashes of the old park now lay. The initial plan was to call it Brush Stadium. Workmen set to the task right away, and enough was in place by August of that same summer for the Giants to come home from Hilltop. However, the name "Polo Grounds" remained in common use among fans, and efforts to officially name the park Brush Stadium went on unsuccessfully for years.

No matter where they played, however, the Giants of 1911 were one of McGraw's great teams, epitomizing the brand of "inside baseball" that McGraw liked to play. The team hit a respectable .279 but was better known for what they would do *after* they reached base.

They would steal.

The 1911 Giants swiped 347 bases, a figure never equaled in modern times. Four regulars, Josh Devore,

Fred Snodgrass, Fred Merkle, and Red Murray, stole sixty-one, fifty-one, forty-nine, and forty-eight bases respectively. Everyone was running. Speed, speed, speed. McGraw loved it and he had built a team upon it. The players did so much sliding on the base paths that team uniforms wore out in midseason and had to be replaced. Once in Chicago, Josh Devore slid into second and couldn't get up because the seat of his uniform had been ripped completely out. In the interest of ragtime-era propriety, his teammates encircled him and led him off the field.

"The 1911 team," McGraw once reflected, "stole the pennant." And that, they did. Of the five base-stealing regulars, Larry Doyle, one of the fastest men on the club, "only" had thirty-eight steals. Why? Doyle was so fast that he ran himself into a league-leading twenty-five triples and a team-leading thirteen home runs, robbing himself of many theft opportunities.

Including Doyle's, the team hit forty-one home runs, but this, too, was a testament to speed, not power, as many were like Doyle's—the inside-the-park variety. And among the forty-one was one round-tripper by Rube Marquard, the only one he would hit in his long career. (An anomaly among pitchers, Marquard was a switch-hitter, like two other future Hall of Famers on the mound, Early Wynn and Robin Roberts.) Rube's home run was probably just a punctuation point. It was the 1911 season that began to change his life, professionally and personally.

Rube had begun to mature. And the work that he and

Uncle Robbie had done in the hot Texas sun in March was starting to pay off. On April 28, Rube pitched an excellent game, his first really good one of the season, shutting down Brooklyn on four hits with eight strike-outs. But the turning point came in May in New York against the St. Louis Cardinals. Mathewson actually started the game in question, but didn't last long. Not for the reason one might suspect, however. After Matty had retired the side in the first, the Giants bombarded St. Louis pitching for thirteen runs in the bottom of the inning. That gave Robbie just the slot he had been in search of for Marquard.

Both Robinson and McGraw felt that Marquard, obviously gifted, needed to work to find his groove and build his confidence. After the thirteen-run outburst, McGraw turned to Mathewson.

"Take the rest of the day off, Matty," McGraw said. "I'm putting in Marquard."

Mathewson would get to save himself for another day, even though he sacrificed an easy victory. But more important for the team, Rube would get to work.

Marquard gave up five runs and twelve hits. But his fastball started to jump. Over the eight innings that he worked, Rube fanned fourteen Cardinals, making many of them look foolish as they flailed after the lanky southpaw's fast stuff. It was an odd and memorable outing. The Giants won a 19–5 laugher and Marquard set an enduring record for most strikeouts in relief.

But most importantly, Rube finally had grasped the confidence he needed to be a major league pitcher. Under Uncle Robbie's tutelage, Marquard now perfected a three-quarter arm delivery from the left side, permanently discarding McGraw's ideas about on overhand delivery. National League hitters responded accordingly. Unable to tell Marquard's sharp curve from his fastball until it was too late, batters found themselves swinging at where they thought the ball would be instead of where it was.

"Rube is now a peach, not a lemon!" proclaimed no less a baseball authority than Mrs. Blanche McGraw, the manager's wife. The missus had a point. And Rube's presence on the staff, creating a 1–2 punch with Mathewson, tipped the balance of power in the league.

On June 28, the Giants returned from exile on Morningside Heights by moving into the partially rebuilt Polo Grounds. Sixteen thousand new seats were available, but only six thousand were sold as the Giants beat the Boston Braves, 3–1.

The date was noteworthy for another reason, too. Outfielder Mike Donlin—that early-day lounge lizard—returned to the major leagues after a two-year absence. Donlin, it will be recalled, had married tiny Mabel Hite in 1906, then left baseball for vaudeville, and finally ended up in Hollywood as a steady supporting actor in silent movies.

McGraw had always had a love-hate affair with Donlin, liking him for his ability and his spirit and loathing him for the way he could drop in and out of baseball. "Donlin was born on Memorial Day and has been parading around ever since," McGraw would once say of his erratic but talented outfielder. Whether or not Donlin related show-biz stories to Marquard during his short stay with the Giants is unknown, but he probably did. In any case, McGraw tired of "Turkey Mike" very quickly and traded him to Boston after twelve appearances with the Giants.

Coincidentally, 1911 was also the season of Charles "Victory" Faust, a sad, mentally incompetent Kansan. One summer afternoon in St. Louis, Faust came out of the grandstand—tall, lanky, wearing a dark suit and a derby hat—and announced to the Giants that a fortune-teller had predicted that he, Faust, would pitch the Giants to a pennant. Faust also alleged that the fortune-teller had predicted that Faust would marry a beautiful girl named Lulu and would be the sire of a long line of baseball heroes.

McGraw asked him to throw a few practice pitches, then hit. It was soon clear that Faust had about as much major league ability as most of the other people in the grandstand, but the Giants had a good laugh. And the team won their series in St. Louis. So the next thing the players knew, Faust was on the train with them on the trip back to New York, courtesy of McGraw, who had adopted Faust as a team mascot and good luck charm.

During this heady time, as the team cruised through the league in first place, the members of the New York Giants also had time to get around the city, making informal appearances, both favorable and unfavorable. One of questionable taste occurred on a day off when Marquard and several other Giants went to Coney Island for an afternoon of recreation.

Among the attractions there was a gallery in an amusement arcade in which "a Negro" was placed on a swing at the end of a long booth. Passersby were invited to throw baseballs at the victim and try to hit him. In keeping with the unsympathetic temper of the times, this was considered entertainment.

The black man didn't show for work the day of the players' visit, but the booth had to open for business. So a white man in blackface — some unfortunate who needed to make a few dollars by ducking baseballs — went onto the swing in his place. The human target proved agile and no one could hit him until the Giants arrived on the scene. A ball was placed in Rube's hand and the young southpaw made just one throw — striking the blackfaced man in the jaw, knocking him unconscious and closing down the booth.

Presumably, in further keeping with the cruelty of the era, everyone had a good laugh except the victim.

The fallout from the $11,000 paid by the Giants to Indianapolis in 1908 for Marquard was still apparent in 1911. Owners complained about the prices paid for — and *to* — ballplayers. Yet they continued to pay them. In that year, the price paid for minor leaguers finally surpassed the sum paid for Marquard. Pittsburgh purchased an entire battery, pitcher Marty O'Toole and catcher Billy Kelly from St. Paul for $22,500. Unfortunately, time would show that the Giants had spent more wisely. O'Toole would win twenty-five of sixty decisions for Pittsburgh over the next four years and Kelly would be nothing more than a backup catcher for parts of two seasons and six games of a third. Such astute talent assessment was perhaps one of the reasons the Pirates would not play in the World Series for another fifteen years.

The Giants, meanwhile, moved away from the Chicago Cubs in August and won the pennant by a comfortable 7 1/2 games. Along the way, Marquard showed further flashes of things to come, such as a game in Pittsburgh in which he struck out six batters in a row, and another one against Boston in which he fanned a total of fourteen. He also showed he could be erratic: in the Boston game, all fourteen whiffs came in the first seven innings. He eventually lost the game 8–7, with an abysmal eighth and ninth frame.

But the ease with which the Giants won the pennant eventually enabled McGraw to activate the team's resident lunatic, mascot Charles "Victory" Faust, and insert him into the final game for one inning against Brooklyn at the new Polo Grounds.

The next day, the *New York Times* described the event as "pure burlesque," as three Brooklyn batters tanked the inning against pitcher Faust. Then, when Faust appeared at the plate, Brooklyn pitchers allowed him to get to first as a hit batter, then steal second, third, and home. The season concluded a few minutes later and the Giants were bound for their first World Series in six years.

And at the end of his first great season, Rube Marquard was showing the talent that McGraw had always believed he had. He led the league in strikeouts with 237. Records of the day also showed that Rube had won twenty-four games and lost only seven, which also gave him the league's best winning percentage. In the

National League, only Grover Cleveland Alexander, with twenty-eight, had won more games.

The 1911 World Series against the Philadelphia Athletics began with much fanfare. It was billed as a rematch of the famous 1905 series, in which Mathewson threw three shutouts and the Giants beat the A's, 4–1. The press of the day also focused on the fact that the series would be played in two of the great new stadia in America, Shibe Park and the newly refurbished Polo Grounds.

The series even managed to nudge another noteworthy news event to the side of the front page, at least in New York and Philadelphia. An aviator named C.P. Rogers was attempting the first transcontinental airplane flight, New York to Pasadena. Rogers took off on September 17 and arrived safely a bit later—on November 5th, making numerous stops and spending eighty-two hours in the air—a quaint cruising speed of thirty miles per hour. Nonetheless, Rogers's aircraft was the first to make the coast-to-coast trip, even though the aviator himself missed a fine World Series.

To create as loud an echo of 1905 as possible, or perhaps to point events toward a similar result, John McGraw decked out his club in sinister black uniforms for the series, as he had done six years before. And again in the opener, Mathewson and the great Charles Albert "Chief" Bender, a Chippewa Indian from Minnesota and the man whom Connie Mack always said was "my greatest money pitcher," would oppose each other on the mound.

What would a World Series in New York be without

media overkill? Not only did the best sportswriters of the day pack the Polo Grounds press box for Game One, but four members of the Giants — McGraw, Meyers, Mathewson, and Marquard — all signed deals with various New York newspapers to "write" daily reports of the games. Connie Mack, Eddie Collins, and Chief Bender struck similar deals with Philly dailies to report their insights on the contests.

Naturally, no athlete was expected to put pen to paper. Ghostwriters were assigned and would fashion articles out of postgame comments, scuttlebutt, and any other coherent thoughts the players may have uttered. But this was long before television or even radio. The World Series was the sporting event of the year in pre–World War I America and newspapers provided the only immediate coverage. The public ate up everything, even hokey columns.

Mathewson beat Bender in Game One, in front of thirty-eight thousand fans in New York on Saturday, October 14. There was no game on Sunday. Monday, the scene shifted to Philadelphia. Marquard pitched for New York, and things began to get interesting.

In the sixth inning of Game Two at Shibe Park, Eddie Collins, the articulate Columbia University graduate who was employed as Connie Mack's second baseman, doubled. Up came Frank Baker, a notorious fastball hitter.

Marquard slipped two of his new curves past Baker. Then, thinking that Baker would be looking for another curve, Marquard tried to strike him out with a fastball.

Big mistake.

Baker lofted the ball over the right field wall for a two-run home run that would eventually win the game for the A's, 3–1. The loss was tough enough for Rube, who was riding high in the New York sports world. But the next day he opened up the *New York American* and found himself being ripped apart under Mathewson's byline. Marquard, Matty's column said, was a fool for laying in a fastball for a hitter like Baker.

There was nothing subtle about the article. The headline read MARQUARD MADE THE WRONG PITCH. The column went on to state — accurately — that manager McGraw had spent a good part of the pregame strategy session warning Rube, and any other pitcher who happened to be paying attention, not to groove a fast one to Baker. Baker had led the American League with eleven home runs in 1911 and was always a threat to hit the ball a long distance.

Despite public protestations to the contrary, Marquard inwardly fumed about being taken to task in print by his roommate. But Mathewson, at whom Marquard now fumed, hadn't even read the article before it was printed. It was wholly a creation of Frank Wheeler, Matty's ghostwriter at the *American*. Nonetheless, Matty was man enough to assume the responsibility for the piece, even though copping a plea might have lessened the tensions on the team. The A's, who enjoyed the article immensely, tacked it to their team bulletin board and had a good collective laugh.

End of the matter? Not by a long shot.

As fate would have it, the next day at the Polo Grounds, Matty was coasting 1–0 against the A's in the ninth inning when—who else?—the same Frank Baker came up to hit in the ninth inning. Big Six appeared to have struck Baker out, but plate umpire Brendan ruled that Baker had ticked the two-strike pitch. Matty tried again, this time with a high fastball. Baker responded with his second home run of the series, a carbon copy of the first one, a friendly high fly over the right-field wall. The homer gave the A's a second life and they won the game in the eleventh. It would prove to be the turning point of the series.

Whatever thoughts went through Marquard's mind when Baker hit his second homer probably couldn't have been printed in any sports section of 1911 or, for that matter, today. Presumably, some of his thoughts took shape, however, and appeared the next afternoon in his own ghostwritten column in the *New York Herald*, which was actually penned by a writer named Frank Menke.

"Will the great Mathewson tell us exactly what he pitched to Baker?" Marquard inquired. "He was present at the same clubhouse meeting at which Mr. McGraw discussed Baker's weakness. Could it be that Matty, too, let go a careless pitch which meant the ball game?"

What effect such sniping had upon the team is difficult to gauge, though it certainly couldn't have done much good. What the roommates Mathewson and Marquard talked about in the moments before curfew was never recorded. The only sure thing was that the big winner was Frank Baker, who would be forever after known as "Home Run" Baker, not for the number of his circuit clouts—although he would lead the American

League four times, he would only hit ninety-four in his career — but rather for the timeliness of two of them.

Following Game Three came the October rains, six days' worth. The series didn't resume until October 24. McGraw started Mathewson and Matty was rusty, allowing four runs and ten hits in seven innings. In the sixth inning, with Matty struggling, McGraw sent Marquard and Hooks Wiltse to the bullpen to warm up. One reporter noted that in the bullpen, "Marquard strolled up and down with a great sardonic grin." Was Rube thinking about those columns? Maybe. Eventually, the A's won 4–2 and now led the series, 3–1.

McGraw came back with Marquard in Game Five. Marquard pitched adequately, though he got burned by three unearned runs. McGraw batted for him, then followed him on the mound with Red Ames and Doc Crandall. The latter got the victory when the Giants fought back with two runs in the ninth inning that tied the game, then pushed one across in the tenth to win.

The winning run was driven in by Fred Merkle, forever the goat of the 1908 season, and, too, it was a weird play. Merkle hit a fly ball to the outfield with Larry Doyle camped on third base. Doyle tagged up, and the throw to the plate by A's right fielder Danny Murphy arrived at the same time as Doyle. But Doyle had come home with an elaborate hook slide that took him past Philadelphia catcher Jack Lapp. Lapp never bothered to tag Doyle, which was a shame from the A's viewpoint. Doyle had slid *past* the plate, but never across it. Umpire Bill Klem made no call and watched in amazement as both teams left the field. Then Klem declared the Giants the winners since the A's had never effected the "out" on Doyle.

McGraw toyed with the idea of coming back with Mathewson on one day's rest in Game Six, but decided against it and started Red Ames. What followed was pure disaster. The A's built up a 6–1 lead against Ames and Wiltse by the sixth inning, then tallied seven more runs in the seventh to ice the game and the series. McGraw had to bring in Marquard in a mop-up role at the end of the game just to get the last two innings finished and get out of Philadelphia.

McGraw was greatly disappointed by his club's failure in the series. But, even in a backhanded way, he did manage to be slyly gracious in defeat. After Game Six, he told Connie Mack that his A's were one of the greatest teams he had ever seen.

"They must be, Connie," he concluded. "I have a great team, too. But you beat us."

McGraw was less civil, however, when he heard that his old Broadway friend George M. Cohan was throwing around a wad of fresh bank notes at the Lambs Club in New York. Cohan had scored a betting coup in the series, picking Philadelphia to win and taking all wagers available from the huge pro-Giant contingent at the Lambs. McGraw considered this a personal betrayal as well as an act of high treason against the city of New York. Cohan won a pile of money, but spent a chilly winter whenever McGraw was in town.

There was also one other footnote to the series, this

one slightly more uplifting. Prior to the 1911 World Series, Connie Mack had taken Chief Bender aside one day. A formal, God-fearing man (most of the time), Mack always addressed Bender by his Christian name.

"Albert?" Mr. Mack asked. "I expect you to win the series for me." He paused. "How much do you owe on your home?"

"None of your business," Bender answered. Eventually, however, Bender admitted that there was still a $3,500 mortgage on his home.

Bender, as has been seen, gave Connie Mack three excellent outings in six games. The day after the 13–2 laugher that ended the series, Mack presented Bender with a bonus check of $3,500 to cover the mortgage.

Soon after the baseball season ended, McGraw took his Giants to Cuba for a brief exhibition tour. Most of the Giants' front line players went on the trip. They voyaged through Jacksonville and Key West before taking a steamer to Havana. The trip was pleasant and successful, though — ballplayers being ballplayers — it was punctuated by a Thanksgiving evening brawl in a Havana cafe that culminated with a trip to the local gendarmerie for McGraw and umpire Cy Rigler.

Among those stars who chose not to travel to Cuba were Merkle, Meyers, and Marquard. Some observers speculated that Marquard was still angry over those columns and wished to be away from the team. Over the years, though, Rube insisted that had not been the case.

"Matty and I both knew that our ghostwriters were just making things lively," Rube insisted decades later. "Reports that said Matty and I were mad at each other and became enemies were just nonsense."

But whatever his reasons may have been for not going to Cuba, Rube had plenty to keep him occupied in New York. Young, single, and handsome, he now had one other quality that had been missing during previous winters.

He was a star athlete. And star athletes had ways of cashing in, as well as hitting all the high spots in a city like New York. The season was barely over when Marquard received a call from vaudeville producer Willie Hammerstein with an offer unlike any he'd ever heard before.

7

◆

A decade into the twentieth century, American show business was still enjoying an era in which anything went, and usually did. And if there was one producer, or promoter, of vaudeville who could make things happen it was Willie Hammerstein, father of Oscar Hammerstein II, the famous composer.

Benjamin Franklin Keith and Edward F. Albee of the Keith-Albee circuit may have owned the buildings and the skeletal operations of vaudeville, but Willie Hammerstein was truly the prince of the night. Hammerstein was a symbol of his era. He understood that show business was a reflection of the lives of ordinary people, all polished up into a performance. And he understood, in a tabloid sense, what people wanted to see and the immediacy with which they wanted to see it.

Hammerstein was one of the great American showmen of this century, and probably the earliest. In 1898, he opened one of the grandest theaters in New York, Hammerstein's Victoria, named, not surprisingly, after his father, Oscar Hammerstein I, who had built the place.

The Victoria flourished for seventeen years under Willie's ownership, grossing more than $20 million and earning Willie Hammerstein a profit of approximately $5 million over that pretax period.

Hammerstein liked to sit in the vast lobby of the theater each night, holding court with friends and business associates, various women, and anyone else who had captured his fancy on that particular day. And what a showman he was! He had many, many legitimately fine acts play at the Victoria. And the number of performers who played the Victoria and grew into stars as a result of Willie Hammerstein's keen eye for talent was immense. But Hammerstein had an even keener eye on the cash register. He knew just how to sprinkle the lurid in with the class acts. And he knew how to sell tickets.

Willie Hammerstein didn't initiate the freak act to the American theater. A thought back to Keith's "chicken with a human face," which played the Keith circuit in the 1890s, would disprove that notion. But Hammerstein did raise the freak act to an art form, at least in terms of promotion.

Hammerstein loved to book wrestlers, bicycle racers, and pugilists. And he had a steady supply of dog acts, pony acts, contortionists, jugglers, and wire walkers. He once had a man with a "seventeen-foot" beard. There were Siamese twins and armless and legless freaks. There was a monkey with a whistle, and darned if the Simian didn't seem as smart as many members of the audience.

Beautiful young milkmaids milking cows were always popular at the Victoria, as were scantily clad "Salome" acts. And anything with an overtly sexual overtone—hopefully linked to a current scandal—was something Hammerstein just had to have. Jack Johnson, the great black heavyweight champion and known paramour of countless white ladies, was a natural for Hammer-stein's Victoria. And when two foxy young New York chorus girls named Lillian Graham and Ethel Conrad fired a few bullets into the leg of a New York socialite named W.E.D. Stokes, Willie Hammerstein hurried over to the local jail, bailed them out, and put them on stage. Stokes was reputed to have been Graham's lover and it can be assumed that it was not Stokes's leg at which she had been aiming. Billed as "The Shooting Stars," Lillian and Ethel stood on the stage of the Victoria and told a packed house—presumably filled with people who had always wanted to shoot a member of the social register—how they had done it. Never mind that they couldn't sing or dance or act. Who cared?

Sharpshooting babes became a subcategory of entertainment and something of a specialty for Willie Hammerstein. Sometime after Lillian and Ethel, Hammerstein signed a woman named Florence Carman who, during a day of vengeful thoughts and raging hormones, shot one of her doctor husband's female patients at the lady's Long Island home. Just to make sure enough sympathy came her way, Flo's act included a mournful, misty-eyed version of a song titled, "Baby Shoes."

Another young lady with a handgun, Evelyn Nesbit, was Hammerstein's hottest act ever. Nesbit was the beautiful bride of Harry Thaw, a millionaire industrialist.

Thaw, enraged by jealousy, murdered Evelyn's former lover, famed architect Stanford White one night in 1906 on the roof of Madison Square Garden. Eventually, Hammerstein brought Evelyn to appear at the Victoria. By happy coincidence, Harry slipped out of jail just as Evelyn was onstage and Hammerstein managed to wrangle a police guard for her from the city. He couldn't have bought such publicity. While she was at the Victoria, she was the most talked about woman in New York.

Hammerstein's ingenuity knew no mortal limits. Or shame. He even booked performers who were dead, like Carmencita, or who didn't even exist, like Count Abdul Kadar.

The dancer named Carmencita had quickened the pulses of male patrons back in the 1890s. She then disappeared. No problem. Hammerstein booked her in the early 1900s at the Victoria, a remarkable accomplishment as Hammerstein personally knew that the original Carmencita had been dead for six years. But for Willie this posed no problem. It fact, her earthly demise *solved* a problem.

Hammerstein tapped an obscure chorus girl who had performed at another house only months earlier. He sent her to Europe and billed her as the original Carmencita from New York. Next he had cables sent back attesting to her current stardom in Europe, just enough to rekindle interest in her. Then he reimported her. No one seemed to mind that she looked a little different. Nor did anyone even notice. Her triumphant reemergence made headlines and great box office.

Then there was the case of Count Abdul Kadar, which

was nothing less than one of the most monumental frauds in American show business.

A country on the verge of revolution, Turkey was big news in 1910. This set Willie thinking about Turks and their sexual mores. A few days later, he dispatched one of his henchmen to Europe to find a Turk with three wives. Or at least, Willie explained to his assistant, find some arrangement that could *pass* for a Turk with three wives. Hammerstein's emissary was a young man named Morris Gest, who later became a very successful Broadway producer in his own right.

In Switzerland, Gest found an artist in a variety house named Adolph Schneider. Schneider did quick oil sketches onstage. Schneider also sort of looked like what people in New York might think a Turk should look like. Gest probably couldn't believe his luck when he went backstage and talked to the artist. Schneider was traveling with his wife, daughter, and sister-in-law.

Gest conferred with the artist and when the conference was over, Schneider had become "Count Abdul Kadar, Court Artist to the Turkish Sultan." Gest then whisked Schneider, that is, Abdul Kadar, over to Adrianople to be outfitted. Heading west again, the act played Paris. Gest started sending cables to America trumpeting the court artist's imminent arrival in New York, where, to everyone's amazement, he was already committed to play Hammerstein's Victoria.

But when Hammerstein went in for a hoax, he went in all the way, never missing an opportunity for free newspaper space. Shortly before the count arrived in New York,

Hammerstein booked the act to stay at the Waldorf-Astoria, where Hammerstein had made equally sure that they would be denied accommodations. Best to keep that *three wives* shtick right out there in public view. In fact, Hammerstein contrived to have the count traipse around Manhattan from one hotel to another with forty pieces of luggage and an equal number of reporters, until the Turk and his *three wives* had been refused lodging just about everywhere and seen by thousands of New Yorkers. Only then did Willie conveniently find an apartment for the Court Artist to the Turkish Sultan and his "harem."

Eventually, the court artist arrived at the Victoria. The show was a hit, even though Schneider's artwork was nothing special and the *three wives* did little more than remove sketches from an easel after the count finished.

And then there were the Cherry Sisters. There was never anything quite like the Cherry Sisters and there probably never will be.

Willie Hammerstein operated on the theory that if he couldn't book a really good act, or couldn't find a really unusual act, then he would present a really bad act. By all admissions, the Cherry Sisters were the worst ever. They were so bad that, well, they were actually *good*, which was the point. Nor was this something that audiences were expected to discover by accident. When Willie booked the Cherrys for a week in 1908, he proudly billed them as "America's Worst Act." And this was one instance in which Hammerstein was not accused of hyperbole.

It had actually been Oscar Hammerstein I who had first booked the Cherrys in the 1890s. But Willie was far from shy about recycling an outstanding "bad" act. And to understand where this one was coming from, one must travel back to a scraggly farm settlement called Marion, Iowa, a few miles from Cedar Rapids, two years before the Victoria was even built.

There were five Cherry Sisters—Addie, Effie, Ella, Jessie, and Lizzie. They were triple-threat ladies. They sang, danced, and emoted, in cliché-ridden dramaturgical efforts of Effie's authorship. They played all the characters in their skits, whether male or female, young or old, repellent or appealing. Their repertoire was so flexible that it could be accommodated to the specific demands of any theatrical occasion.

In vaudeville, at Oscar Hammerstein's Olympia and later at Willie Hammerstein's Victoria, they played twenty-minute turns. But over the course of their careers they also supplied a full evening's entertainment in legitimate theaters, opera houses, lodge halls, fire houses, tents, church basements, and—in the Midwest—lofts above feed stores.

A full evening—and it sure was—would begin with a quintet rendition of what the sisters called a "glad" song, such as "Sweet Alice Ben Bolt." Then there would be a play, billed as "a dramatic thunderbolt," such as *The Gypsy's Warning*. The night would then conclude with a "sad" song, "Curfew Must Not Ring Tonight." All of this work was of Effie's authorship. And why the sisters would want to start their audiences off "glad" but send them home "sad" is another matter.

In 1893, when the Cherrys began their careers, the

sisters ranged in age from middle teens to middle twenties. Effie, the middle sister, and the most aggressive and articulate of the five, was twenty-one. Effie Cherry had certainly not been favored by nature. Her face had equine contours, her body was short and thick, and she had what one reviewer once called "a belligerent stance and a chin to go with it." In truth, the sum total of Effie's appearance was no better and no worse than any of her sisters. "About the only thing that could be said for them was that they didn't wear glasses," remarked another reviewer. Modern observers might have noted the uncanny resemblance that Sister Addie bore to Miss Olive Oyl of the *Popeye* comic strip.

Aside from amateur performances in their home hamlet, the Cherrys' first noteworthy performance came at Green's Opera House in Cedar Rapids, usually a one-night stop for touring vaudeville companies. As it happened, an election campaign had just ended and many of Green's patrons were in possession of horns that they had used in a victory celebration.

The Charming Cherrys flounced onto the stage in red-and-white calico dresses that they had made themselves, while a pianist in the pit vamped until the ladies were ready. Then the sisters burst into a strident off-key rendition of "Alice Ben Bolt."

Next followed the one-act play, *The Gypsy's Warning.*

In this work, Effie, the author, socked home the message that the loss of a woman's virginity prior to marriage was a fate worse than death. In this drama, an early-day wolf—portrayed by Sister Addie because of her deep voice — had lecherous designs upon an unsullied maiden — portrayed by Lizzie — who was warned against the wolf's advances by a gypsy — with Jessie playing the title role.

Addie, in the wolf's role, was for some reason dressed as a Spanish cavalier, complete with knee breeches that revealed her spavined limbs. She had leered just once at the virtuous maiden (Lizzie) when high up in the second balcony a devotee of fine drama blew a horn. Someone in the first balcony tittered. An orchestra patron guffawed. Feet began to stomp. Soon everyone who had a horn was blowing it. Others were yelling, hooting, stomping, or whistling.

The sisters stepped out of character, grouped themselves on the apron of the stage, and bowed in response to what they actually believed was tumultuous approval. The play resumed. When it came to a point where the Spanish cavalier (Addie) hissed through a wax mustache, the cacaphony began anew. And once more the Cherrys stepped out of character to acknowledge audience reaction. It went that way not just for the rest of the evening, but for *the next three years*.

The sisters went to Chicago and found a booking agent who kept a straight face when they auditioned and sent them throughout the Midwest on the Chautauqua circuit, a series of tents and revival halls throughout the heartland that attempted to bring religion and entertainment to the hinterlands. William Jennings Bryan, who gave temperance lectures, was perhaps the best known name on the bills. Edgar Bergen, future partner to Charlie

McCarthy and eventual father to Candice Bergen, was the young performer who went farthest. In any case, audiences on the circuit were *very* forgiving. In three years on the tour, the Cherrys were never exposed to adverse criticism. Then Oscar Hammerstein caught the act in his travels one night and, well, couldn't believe it. So he signed the girls to play New York.

Cruel? Absolutely. But this was show biz.

On their opening night on Broadway, the Cherry Sisters minced out awkwardly in those very same calico dresses that they had worn in their Iowa debut three years earlier. No sooner had the Manhattan audience caught its breath than the sisters launched into a "sad" song entitled, "She was My Sister and Oh How I Miss Her."

The voices of the ladies took turns in cracking. The rendition, according to all reviewers, was incredibly ghastly. By the time the last note of the song was sent twanging on its way, there was hardly a dry eye in the house. The audience was beside itself with laughter.

Next the Cherrys went into a dance. This, too, was something to behold. The ladies collided, got separated, were constantly out of step, stopped to adjust their coiffures, and did just about everything else they shouldn't have done except fall into the orchestra pit.

Then the Cherrys recited a message about virginity, complete with gestures totally unrelated to the subject. The moral message was followed by a "glad" song titled "Three Cheers for the Railroad Boys." That closed the act. The audience was so laughed out that it began to applaud. When the sisters retired to the wings, hot and flushed with excitement, they were convinced that they were a resounding success.

And actually they were.

Word got around the city. People came out in droves to see the ladies from Iowa. Then the first dark shadow fell across their paths. On the third night of their appearance at the Olympia, someone in the balcony threw a tomato onto the stage. Soon the air was alive with cabbages, apples, eggs, bunches of radishes, and even sandwiches. The barrage was so heavy that the Cherrys fled to the wings.

Hammerstein, not wishing to lose a good act for six weeks, consoled the girls. He explained to the sisters, whose naïveté was in inverse proportion to their talent, that the barrage of edibles was a resounding symbol of success. It was, he said, the work of paid agents of established stars jealous of the new competition. And they actually believed this.

So the next night—and ever after—the Cherrys performed behind a net that the producers had conveniently strung across the stage for their act alone. The net idea was not new. In the 1880s a lawyer named James Owen O'Connor threw away his law books and aspired to be a Shakespearean actor. Like the Cherrys, he was so bad that he was good, and thus became the first performer of record to work behind a net. For their part, the Cherrys were so convinced by Oscar Hammerstein's explanation of events, and so conditioned against facing the facts of life, that they came to measure the success of a performance by the volume of produce stopped by the net.

Not only did they complete their six-week tour, but on the strength of their initial Broadway success, the Cherrys received bookings for years in large variety houses in Boston, Philadelphia, Washington, Baltimore, and Chicago, as well as all the smaller cities in between. They received between $100 and $200 a week, which was no small bit of change. And they traveled with the net, which became standard equipment for them. What Oscar Hammerstein had brought to fame at the Olympia was just one more act that Willie was happy to resurrect at the Victoria, as circumstances might allow.

As for the actual Victoria Theater, performers loved to play it and audiences loved to visit it. But Willie couldn't leave well enough alone. He had to add two P.T. Barnum-style touches.

On hot summer days, he sought to have paying patrons cool down at the Victoria. To encourage this, he mounted a huge thermometer in the lobby. Supposedly, the thermometer indicated the temperature within the theater. But the bottom of the thermometer rested on a block of ice, carefully concealed under a cloth. A sign in the lobby usually indicated that the temperature was seventy degrees or cooler.

"If you don't believe it—look at the thermometer!" proclaimed a nearby sign.

Once drawn into the theater, patrons were urged to visit the roof garden, another opportunity to spend money. Ingeniously, Hammerstein had heated the elevator that took patrons to the roof. When they stepped out, the sweating customers were convinced that it *was* cooler up there, even if it wasn't.

Hammerstein, as noted earlier, was also a specialist at drawing the sporting crowd into his theater. So it was not any surprise that Rube Marquard's initiation into show business — following his 1911 World Series appearance — was not long in coming. Nor was it any surprise that it came from Hammerstein.

A pert, pretty, dark-haired woman named Annie Kent was a middle-range star in 1911. Like many women of the vaudeville stage, she could sing, dance, and do light comedy. In later years, the so-called "mixed act," a man and a woman, developed a certain formula, with the man being the "straight" and the woman being the "comic." Some of this stuff was pretty basic. And banal. But it worked for the audiences.

A sample:

MAN
(looking at her)
Say, you look great! Tell me
about yourself.

WOMAN
Well, I'm Helen Summer.

MAN
I'll bet you're great in winter, too!

There were many successful partnerships, both long term and short. George Burns and Gracie Allen were probably the slickest act to evolve from this formula.

On short notice, in November 1911, Marquard received an invitation from Hammerstein to formulate a "mixed act" with Miss Kent. Rube agreed, though he didn't have much to do other than stand on stage, feed Annie some lines, let the audience see him in person, and try not to trip when she started to dance with him.

Nonetheless, the act—billed as Rube Marquard & Annie Kent—played a full fourteen minutes at Hammerstein's Victoria, that mecca of sports-and-show biz fusion. By this time, there was no novelty of a ballplayer being onstage. Mathewson and Meyers, after all, had played at that theater the previous year. And Donlin & Hite were still packing crowds in a few blocks away. So the ho-hum skepticism of the public was not far from the reviewer's mind when *Variety* covered Rube Marquard's world premiere as a performer.

> Baseball players are no longer stellar attractions in New York vaudeville,

wrote the *Variety* critic.

> The first to reach here used up all the cream. A number of people walked out of Hammerstein's Monday night before Marquard made his appearance at 10:28. Pretty late, of course, but still the Giants

$11,000 pitcher is to be taken seriously.
Annie Kent did what was practically a
singing single and dancing specialty. For
a finish, they do a few steps together — or
rather Rube took one step to each three of
Miss Kent's.

Rube, in other words, wasn't bad. Most observers said
he was surprisingly good, though he had little to do. And
his performance did not escape the notice of other actors
and agents. Nor, as the act ran through the Christmas
season and into the beginning of the new year, did Rube
miss out on one of the fringe benefits of a star of stage
and athletic field.

After a few performances, he and Miss Kent were an
item around town, leaving the theater together each night
and constantly being seen at the trendy places in Manhattan. Rube had progressed quite well for a frightened
young man barely out of his teens. He now had a toe-
hold in two worlds of entertainment and was squiring a
Broadway actress around town as well. And the best years
of his life were now approaching the horizon.

Of course, if Rube had a romance going with Annie
Kent, and a honeymoon going with the New York fans,
he wasn't the only one in parallel circumstances. Blossom Seeley had both going, too, although in a different
way. On October 1, 1911, in Jersey City, New Jersey, Seeley
and Joe Kane were married. Now everything was set for
the explosive year of 1912. But there was just one final
footnote to 1911.

Rube and Annie Kent were climbing into a horse-drawn carriage in the theater district one night when an apparent stranger accosted Rube.

"The stranger appeared to be in genuine hard luck," reported the *New York Telegraph*, as they recorded the incident. "And as Marquard was in no special hurry, he stopped to converse with the man."

As it turned out, the man was the same one whose jaw Marquard had blasted with a baseball the previous summer at Coney Island.

"The sensation I experienced I cannot describe," the man told Rube. "I was unconscious for two hours. So I do know that you must have a punch that could do some mischief with some of the pugilists around town."

Rube couldn't quite figure where this conversation was going until the downtrodden one announced that he wanted to arrange a boxing match between Marquard "and a heavyweight who is training in the Bronx." In exchange, all he needed was a dollar to get him through the evening.

Rube smiled and, perhaps feeling a trifle guilty over the Coney Island incident, dug into his pocket for a silver dollar. He gave it to the stranger and hopped into the carriage with Miss Kent.

No heavyweight match was ever arranged. And Rube never saw the stranger—or the dollar—again.

8

—◆—

Seeley, managed adroitly now by her new husband, Joe Kane, quickly built upon the New York success that had come to her from her role in *The Hen-Pecks*. Good roles in musicals were hers almost for the asking. But after leaving the Lew Fields production at the Broadway Theater, Seeley was steered back to vaudeville—where the paychecks were bigger—by her ever-watchful agent-husband.

This was no small professional gamble. There were plenty of single female acts in New York. So to headline, where the top money was, a woman had to be good. Very good. Seeley was.

In April 1912, she challenged the demonic audiences at the Colonial Theater, home of the infamous claque that would drive performers from the stage with the rhythmic clapping.

She survived.

> Miss Blossom Seeley, who has quit the Winter Garden for vaudeville,

wrote the critic in the *Billboard*,

is one of the few single women with a
name now playing the two-a-day houses
who can make good on her merit alone. A
breezy personality and girlish looks
coupled with good material and an ability to use it, made her act one of the pleas-
ing features of the bill.

The same critic was also enthusiastic about the Phila-
delphia-born thirty-three-year-old comic who followed,
the former William Claude Dukenfield:

W.C. Fields, the tramp juggler, fresh from
European triumphs, is easily the peer of
any comedy juggler in vaudeville. He repeated his former success and was warmly
welcomed back to America.

Five weeks later, still sharpening her act, Seeley went
to Hammerstein's where she again knocked the audiences
dead. She had three new songs and "got each one over,"
said *Variety*. She continued to introduce and popularize
the new song, "Standing On The Levee Waiting for the
'Robert E. Lee'," and included it in a ten-minute program
of finger-snapping syncopated ragtime tunes, a style of
singing and music that would become as much of a trademark as "Robert E. Lee."

"This act will be a Number One!" *Variety* thundered.

Soon after, she toured the country. Kane secured for
her a starring role in a show titled, *The Charity Girl*, and

more excellent reviews followed for Seeley, from New York all the way west to Chicago. But the show itself was not well received.

During 1912 various reform movements took hold in the country, notably several civic-minded undertakings to "clean up" America's teeming slums. *The Charity Girl* carried with it a message—albeit a strange one—that the reform movement was "making bums" out of the residents of New York's Lower East Side. Seeley played a "Bowery girl," named Becky, and obviously the show was meant to grab the audience by the lapels and shake them. In one song called "Charity," which Seeley sang, there came a line that the *New York Telegraph* called "intended as a shocker (but which is) . . . unprintable in a self-respecting journal and which should be unsingable in any playhouse."

Apparently, much of the audience felt the same way and the show did not last long. Blossom was off to Chicago where one Windy City performance even made news back in New York. Seeley, in the midst of an intense dance number, stepped on a nail so sharp that it penetrated her slippers. She kept dancing, until she dramatically danced offstage, where a burly stagehand pulled the nail loose. Then she was back on, to heavy applause.

"I never stood still," Blossom recalled years later, speaking of her changing routines as much as of her footwork on stage. "I was always looking for new material and new ideas. I was always ready to work with something completely new."

Everything seemed to be going fine for the Kanes. If there were a cloud on the horizon at all, it emanated from Joe. Married only a few months, Joe was so smitten with Blossom that he could barely stand to have other men look at her, much less speak to her. The marriage had not been perfect so far. Kane, after all, was a man given to fits of extreme temper and rage, something Blossom had not known when she married him.

But always in the forefront was the search for ways to move his top client from the good money, which she was now making, to the really fantastic money that could be reaped in vaudeville.

He was well aware of what Christy Mathewson had been earning the previous autumn ($1,000 a week for fifteen weeks). There were rumors that McGraw was on the verge of cutting a deal for personal appearances, a deal accelerated by the Little Napoleon's many Broadway friends. And everyone along the Great White Way knew the money that Donlin and Hite were making.

It didn't take Kane long to begin thinking about how much he could make with Blossom if he teamed her with a star athlete and devised a first-class musical skit for them. As the summer of 1912 progressed, Joe studied the sports pages carefully, looking to see who that athlete might be.

The Giants trained in Marlin, Texas, again in the spring of 1912, and were heavily favored to win another pennant. Much of the baseball world savored the possibility of another fall matchup between McGraw's Giants and

Connie Mack's A's, the heavy favorite to take the American League crown again. Spring training over, the defending National League champion Giants opened the 1912 season in Brooklyn under circumstances that would be memorable in more ways than one.

First, there was the game. At aging Washington Park, the Giants walloped the home club, 18–3. Then there was the overflow crowd from the grandstand that was allowed onto the field behind ropes, but by the third inning, the ropes were gone. Fly balls, fans, and outfielders seemed to converge at the same place, and, as would be increasingly common over the years that followed, a large number of fights broke out in the stands between New York fans and Brooklyn fans. After six innings, umpire Bill Klem called the game to prevent injuries to the fans, the players, and the park.

The winning pitcher for the Giants was Marquard, who started and finished the truncated affair. Eight days later, back in Manhattan, the Giants formally dedicated their new enlarged and redesigned Polo Grounds. That day, too, included a victory over Brooklyn.

By May 15, the Giants moved into first place. By July 4, they were 54–12. They would stay at the top of their circuit till the end of the season, comfortably winning a second consecutive pennant with a ten-game margin over the Pirates.

But the big story that season was Marquard. Rube won on opening day and won his next start after that. And the next one, too. It was a time when the twenty-one-year-old southpaw would silence his critics forever.

On July 3, Marquard beat Brooklyn yet again, raising his year's record to nineteen wins and no losses. From April to July, the entire sports watched Marquard compile and add to his streak. Nineteen straight! The streak did not end until July 8 in New York when Jimmy Lavender of Chicago defeated New York, 7–2.

"Actually," Marquard told Lawrence Ritter half a century later, "I won twenty straight, not nineteen, but because of the way they scored then, I didn't get credit for one of them. I relieved Jess Tesreau in the eighth inning of a game one day with the Giants behind, 3–2. In the ninth inning, Heinie Groh singled and Art Wilson homered and we won, 4–3. But they gave (starting pitcher Jess) Tesreau credit for the win instead of me."

Marquard was correct. In 1912, the official scorer would award wins to almost any starting pitcher who lasted more than seven innings, no matter how the game was won. Under current scoring rules, Marquard *would* have received credit for twenty wins in a row. What he never pointed out as years went by, however, was that he also *gained* two wins under the old scoring system that would have been "saves" in modern times.

Nonetheless, the record has stood for eighty-four years so far, and would have stood equally long had it been either eighteen wins or twenty.

Most of the games weren't even close:

April 11	Giants	18	Brooklyn	3
April 16	Giants	8	Boston	2
April 24	Giants	11	Philadelphia	4

May 1   Giants 11   Philadelphia 4 (Relieved)
May 7   Giants 6   St. Louis 2
May 11   Giants 10   Chicago 3
May 16   Giants 4   Pittsburgh 1
May 20   Giants 3   Cincinnati 0
May 24   Giants 6   Brooklyn 3
May 30   Giants 7   Philadelphia 1
June 3   Giants 8   St. Louis 3
June 8   Giants 6   Cincinnati 2
June 12   Giants 3   Chicago 2 (Relieved)
June 17   Giants 5   Pittsburgh 4 (11 innings)
June 19   Giants 6   Boston 5 (Relieved)
June 21   Giants 5   Boston 2
June 25   Giants 2   Philadelphia 1
June 29   Giants 8   Boston 6
July 3   Giants 2   Brooklyn 1
July 7 defeated by Chicago, 7–2

Rube registered a rather unusual complaint directly after the game he finally lost to the Cubs. Reports of the day told of a "lunatic woman" named Mary Porter who was hanging from a tree outside the Polo Grounds during the game. She spent most of the game screaming at Marquard and rooting for the Cubs. To writers after the game, Marquard complained about a "jinx" and indicated that he had been unnerved by Crazy Mary.

During the course of the streak, Rube pitched sixteen complete games, was relieved twice, and won a game in relief on June 19 against Boston. He also had one "no decision" on a start that Mathewson eventually lost in relief. And when the streak ended, Rube had allowed only forty-nine runs in twenty games.

In winning nineteen straight games, Marquard set a single season consecutive game winning record that remains until this day. Two decades later, another Giant, Carl Hubbell, would win twenty-six games in a row over the course of the 1933–34 seasons, but Hubbell's streak is barely remembered by professional baseball.

Marquard's nineteen in a row is recognized as a modern record, though a thorough look in the record books will turn up the name of yet another Giant pitcher, Tim Keefe, who won nineteen straight in 1888. Keefe, a contemporary of John Montgomery Ward, pitched when the pitcher's mound was only fifty feet from home plate, instead of the sixty feet six inches that it is in modern times, thus creating a greater advantage for the pitcher. Keefe also was credited with a win that he would not have had under modern scoring rules. So conceivably, Marquard could have had twenty straight, and Keefe only eighteen.

Rube's winning streak made him a nationally known, front-page celebrity. Soon everyone wanted a piece of him. And Rube was making sure that everyone who could pay for a piece could get one.

One of the most interesting offers to come his way was from an early film studio called the Kalem Company. Kalem produced one-reel silent movies, and they churned out a nearly inexhaustible batch of them. The sun rarely set on Kalem's efforts. In 1912 they were one of the most active film production companies in the world. Kalem had California units busy in Santa Monica and Glendale. They also had part of their company in New York and New Orleans, as well as a surprisingly busy outpost in Jacksonville, Florida. Abroad, they shot films in Egypt, the Holy Land, and Ireland. Their writers, directors, actors, and crew rarely had a day of rest.

In 1910, a New York photographer and cameraman named L.E. Taylor photographed a young woman named Alice Joyce for a series of newspaper advertisements. Knowing how photogenic she was, Taylor brought her to the attention of Kalem executives. The executives liked what they saw. How could anyone not? Looking for a way to exploit Marquard's sudden fame during the summer of 1912 when his long winning streak was the toast of the sports world, Kalem teamed Marquard with Joyce.

Alice Joyce was a beauty of quiet, patrician elegance. She had abundant brown hair and dark expressive eyes. A genuinely radiant young woman, she was exactly the same age as Rube.

"She underplayed her scenes," wrote one critic in *Films in Review* much later in Alice's career, "and as long as the camera featured her eyes, there was never any doubt of what she was thinking."

She would go on to be a considerable star of the silent screen and early talkies. Her career ranged from something called *The Trail of The Pomos Charm* in 1911 (in which she played an Indian maiden in love with a white man) to her final feature, a talkie named *He Knew Women* in 1930. The latter film was a screen adaptation of the S. N. Behrman play titled *The Second Man*, a production that had starred Alfred Lunt and Lynn Fontanne on Broadway. In the film, Alice Joyce played the Fontanne role.

Joyce's career, which was actually very much of a pioneering one for an American screen actress, would be divided into three parts: Her early films with Kalem, after having been one of the top fashion models in New York; her middle years at Vitagraph, and the latter years from 1923 to 1930, when she was a much admired freelancing leading lady. She was just forty when she finished her career, and many observers say that she was an even more beautiful woman then than when younger. But then, as now, good roles for women over forty were rare.

Nonetheless, in July 1912, Kalem was ready to roll with a star vehicle for Marquard. Lest anyone miss the idea, the name of this silent one-reeler was *Rube Marquard Wins.*

The plot? There was "a bit of a clever" story line, commented the *Moving Picture World* on August 17, 1912, one week before the film's release in New York.

Here's how it went:

Miss Joyce attends a game at the Polo Grounds where, like any other single woman in attendance, she happens to meet "the champ," Rube Marquard, who plays himself. A few days later, he gets in touch with her and invites her to attend a morning practice of the New York Giants. Plenty of swooning here. She decides to accept the invitation.

The star pitcher in the nation has time before the game to usher Miss Joyce onto the field — plenty of shots of the Polo Grounds grandstand filled with fans at this point —

whereupon he shows her how he throws his various pitches. She looks on with great interest. Then back to a choice box seat with her.

"Now the plot deepens," noted the *Moving Picture World*.

Gamblers approach Rube Marquard after the game and attempt to bribe him to "let up" in the next big contest. A paragon of virtue, Rube hauls off and belts the dude who made the suggestion.

But all is not resolved. Another of the conspirators telephones Marquard and informs him that he, the conspirator, is handling some of Marquard's investments. Marquard must come to the Metropolitan Tower in Manhattan just before the important ball game. For some reason, Rube falls for this. The gamblers then lock him in a room so that he will not be able to pitch in the important ball game.

Alice to the rescue!

As it turns out, Alice just happens to be living in a hotel not far from the Metropolitan Tower. She suddenly remembers that she is to attend the game at the Polo Grounds that day. She apparently does not own a clock or a watch because she looks out her hotel room window at the clock on the Metropolitan Tower to see if she still has time to get to the game.

She sees a man waving a towel from a room below the clock. Intrigued, she fetches a handy pair of binoculars, trains them on the Metropolitan building, and — surprise! — recognizes the national hero who befriended her a few days earlier.

A dialogue board is seen on the screen:

> Now what can Marquard be doing in the
> Tower at this time of day?

she wonders.

> She consults the morning newspaper. More dialogue.

> Yes, Rube is to pitch today! He should be
> at the Polo Grounds at this very moment!

Alice decides to investigate. She runs down the stairs of the hotel and out into the street. She jumps into a new automobile, presumably one that she owns. She drives to the Metropolitan Tower where she talks the building superintendent into breaking into the room in question and freeing the National League's premier starting pitcher.

Then she and Rube motor to the ballpark. A parking place awaits them in front of the ball field. No one seems to get upset as they rush through the gates without a ticket. Rube grabs a baseball, goes out to the mound, and foils the opposing team. The gamblers lose big.

In the final scene, that evening at the hotel, Rube is all dolled up in evening clothes and Alice wears a gown. They dine together. Several other players from the Giants appear to present Alice with a huge bouquet and a card of thanks. They could not have won that day without her.

As a vehicle, *Rube Marquard Wins* was primitive. But it was also successful, drawing good notices for Rube, who didn't have to stretch much to play himself, as well as for Alice Joyce. The film, itself, even received good notices. An actor named Maurice Costello, who would later have a long and distinguished film career, supported the two leads.

But the distractions of being a celebrity, much less a film star, were starting to take their toll on Rube. He led the league in wins with twenty-six and posted a creditable 26–11 record, good for the third-highest winning percentage in the National League. A closer examination, of course, reveals that after the first nineteen wins, Rube was only 7–11 in his last eighteen decisions. Perhaps it proved the old adage that a man can only excel at one national sport at a time.

The Giants won 103 games in 1912, but sometimes it was difficult to see exactly how they had been *that* much better than the also-rans. True, they did have plenty of the more subtle components that appear in box scores, such as superb pitching and excellent speed (319 stolen bases) and defense. But they did not have a single outstanding day-to-day player, even though they scored 823 runs, the most in the National League since 1899. Very quietly, they also led the league in home runs with forty-seven, less than one every three games.

They also did not have one more shot at the Philadelphia A's in the fall classic. Instead, they found waiting for them in the World Series an upstart squad from

Boston, which had brought that city its first American League title since 1904, the year John McGraw refused to play them.

The Red Sox had run away with the American League pennant, finishing fourteen games in front of second place Philadelphia. The Red Sox were a team that was strong at every position, but particularly strong because they had perhaps the greatest everyday outfield of all time — Duffy Lewis, Tris Speaker, and Harry Hooper. On the mound was Marquard's old opponent from the day he was showcased in Indianapolis — Smoky Joe Wood, who had graduated from the American Association to be, this year, a splendid thirty-four-game winner for the BoSox.

As is the case whenever a New York team plays a Boston team, this World Series was an Event, with loyal fans of each team parading through the opposing city on the days of games. For the series, which started on October 7, the Giants wore new violet-trimmed uniforms, which McGraw — an eighth grade dropout — had chosen out of his fondness for New York University teams.

McGraw tried to gain an advantage on the Sox by pitching his rookie, Jeff Tesreau (17–7) in Game One, then coming back with Mathewson and Marquard in Games Two and Three, respectively. The strategy backfired when Smoky Joe Wood outpitched Tesreau, 4–3 and put the BoSox out to a lead in the series.

Mathewson pitched the second game and pitched well, the first World Series game ever played at Boston's new Fenway Park. Matty was undone, however, by five Giant errors that created four unearned runs. The game went eleven innings and was eventually called on account of darkness, the first World Series game to ever end in a tie.

Marquard pitched Game Three and was back in the form that had taken him to nineteen straight wins earlier in the season. He scattered five hits over the first eight innings and didn't allow a run until one out in the ninth. The Giants won, 2–1, to tie the series. Rube walked one and struck out six in the complete game victory.

Wood beat Tesreau again in Game Four and Hugh Bedient beat a very unlucky Christy Mathewson in Game Five, Mathewson losing 2–1 due partially to poor fielding at shortstop by Larry Doyle.

That brought the series back to the Polo Grounds with the Sox leading 3–1 and Marquard again on the mound. Again Rube gave the Giants the win they needed, allowing no earned runs in a 5–2 Giant win. Rube now had the only two New York wins in the series. He would not appear again in this World Series, despite a 2–0 record and an 0.50 ERA.

The action then moved back to Boston and Jeff Tesreau finally beat Smoky Joe Wood in the third matchup between the two pitchers. It was a wild, sloppy game with seven errors between the two clubs and punctuated by a strange home run—under the ground rules of the day—that Larry Doyle hit on one hop over the low right field fence in Fenway.

A crowd of 17,034 assembled for Game Eight (one tie, remember) on October 16 at Fenway. It would prove to be one of the most heartbreaking losses in New York sports history.

The great Mathewson took a 1–1 tie into the tenth inning in Boston. Then the Giants appeared to have the game won when Merkle singled in the top of the tenth to drive in Red Murray from second base.

In the bottom of the tenth, however, pinch hitter Clyde Engel began the inning by lofting an easy fly ball to Giant centerfielder Fred Snodgrass. It was as easy a fly ball as a major league outfielder would ever see. And Snod-grass muffed it, letting the ball fall from his glove. Engel went to second on the play.

Snodgrass made some amends by making a sensational catch in deep right field on Harry Hooper's long drive, although Engel, the tying run, went to third base. But then Mathewson walked the weak-hitting Steve Yerkes, bringing up the ever dangerous Tris Speaker with runners on first and third.

Speaker lofted an easy pop-up to the first base coach's box. Inexplicably, first baseman Fred Merkle — the "goat" of the 1908 season — stepped aside and watched the ball. Chief Meyers the catcher raced down the line and made an attempt to catch it and Matty ran over from the mound, also. But the ball dropped safely to the ground.

Given a second life, Speaker singled in Clyde Engel with the tying run. After Duffy Lewis was intentionally walked, Larry Gardner sent a long fly to left. Josh Devore ran it down but was unable to throw out Yerkes, whose free trip around the bases brought Boston a world championship. Some of the New York writers in the press box sat with tears in their eyes as Mathewson stoically walked off the field with the toughest loss of his career. In this series, Mathewson had pitched three complete games, 28.2 innings, had an ERA of 1.26, and had nothing to show for it except an 0–2 record. Not entirely unrelated to Mathewson's disappointing fate, the Fred Snodgrass muff to start the bottom of the tenth inning became part of baseball folklore.

Jimmy Durante used to split up audiences with the famous line, "Everybody's trying to get in on the act." Durante was only nineteen years old in 1912 and had not yet coined his signature phrase. But the notion might never have been more true. After the baseball season of 1912 ended, everyone seemed to want to get into the act.

Charlie Dooin of the Phillies sang again with Dumont Minstrels in the Quaker City. Larry Doyle took a role as the villain in a melodrama. Doc White, the songwriter who'd composed a hit with Ring Lardner, joined with three other Chicago players to form a quartet. Not to be outdone, four Red Sox players did exactly the same, calling themselves the Boston Red Sox Quartette.

Shortstop Joe Tinker of the Cubs, forever immortalized as Tinker-to-Evers-to-Chance (completely ignoring third baseman Harry Steinfelt, who was probably their equal) was doing even better in show business. Tinker had done several seasons in vaudeville and was improving his stage skills each year. The *New York Telegraph* reviewed his skit, *A Great Catch* as "a clever little piece" which "deserved" the keen audience reaction that followed it. The *Chicago Journal* lavished even more praise, calling Tinker "a refreshing change from most athletic

champions who took to the stage. . . . (He is) good looking, bore himself like a gentleman, and neither clumsy
nor obstreperous."

Among those highly impressed with Tinker's reviews
was Tinker himself, who now in 1912 signed for another
vaudeville tour, primarily in New York and Chicago, and
announced his retirement for the 1913 season. Eventually Tinker would change his mind and he would become the playing manager of the Cincinnati Reds. His
career with the Cubs, however, was essentially finished,
except for one hit in ten at-bats in 1916, after a two-year
stint in the Federal League.

The best offer of the postseason, however, came to
John McGraw.

McGraw's theatrical agent, M.S. Bentham, secured for
the Giant manager a ten-week run on the rich B.T. Keith
circuit, calling for a staggering $3,000 per week. An ac-
curate barometer of just how much money that was
would be to consider that McGraw was the highest paid
manager in baseball at $18,000 per year. Ten weeks on
the stage almost doubled his baseball salary.

Bozeman Bulger, the baseball writer of the *New York
Evening World* (which, it will be recalled, never ripped a
Keith show) concocted a twelve-minute skit of material —
anecdotes, reminiscences, and a monologue addressing
"the hitherto carefully guarded secrets of inside baseball,
as perfected by the New York Giants."

McGraw opened at the Colonial on November 1. He
made his appearance in a black evening coat with tails,
white tie, a black-and-white-striped vest, and gray trou-

sers — a McGraw barely recognizable to a city used to seeing him in a Giants uniform at the Polo Grounds. McGraw
was used to standing before twenty-five to forty thousand
enemy baseball fans, having them howl at him, and never
give it a second thought. Yet he confided to friends that
the prospects of facing a full theater — and the notoriously
tough Colonial, at that — set his Gaelic heart to leaping.

"It was a daily reminder that I have nerves," McGraw
told one writer in a Bronx theater later on in the tour.
And perhaps there was some significance to the fact that
McGraw arrived at the theater for his debut performance
just five minutes before he was scheduled to go on.

Nonetheless, McGraw proved an enormous success,
both on the stage and at the box office, despite having
only memorized his material a day or two beforehand.
He adhered — sort of — to the script that Bozeman Bulger
had prepared for him and told four or five baseball stories to a highly receptive crowd of New York sports fans.
He started by assuring them that he did not blame Fred
Snodgrass for the loss of the World Series and that
Snodgrass would return for the 1913 season. "The stories were bright and surprisingly well told," remarked
Variety in giving the Giants' manager an excellent notice.

Even the attempts at humor seemed to work, though
the question of taste doesn't completely survive to the
present day.

"Do you remember Dummy Taylor?" McGraw asked
the audience. "One day he was 'talking' (in sign language)
to another deaf and dumb mute and he was holding his

hand under his coat as he was talking. I said I wonder what Dummy is telling the other fellow. Then one of my players said, 'Oh, Dummy is telling a risqué story.'"

The audience actually liked that one.

On opening night, patrons also received an extra treat, as Christy Mathewson and his wife Jane appeared in a special box to witness the performance. During the applause following McGraw's appearance, members of the audience clamored for something from the great Big Six. Mathewson obliged with a short speech from his box, stopping the night's show. The phrase, "a tough act to follow," would have to have been coined with such situations in mind. Such other acts that shared a bill with McGraw were "Zeno, the Human Fly," "Doodle & Shuffle," a song-and-dance team, and "Ione, the Girl with the Doughnut Eyes."

The Colonial sold out and scalpers had most of the best tickets for McGraw's entire run. The only unhappy note was the death from illness on November 11 of John T. Brush, the Giants owner and a close friend of the manager.

McGraw went quickly out to Indianapolis where the Brush family had built its fortune as dry goods merchants, and where Brush was to be buried. McGraw delivered the eulogy at his friend's funeral, served as a pallbearer, and traveled back to New York to maintain his two-a-day matinee-and-evening performance schedule. Upon Brush's death, controlling interest in the Giants passed to Harry Hemstead, Brush's son-in-law, who up until then had learned everything he knew about baseball by managing the family clothing store in Indianapolis.

McGraw's vaudeville tour was a resounding success. But that didn't mean he was the only hot act on the stage. Also on the bill with McGraw — later in the tour — was one of the best "water nymph" acts of the day, "Odiva, the Goldfish Lady." In a small way, McGraw found himself upstaged in a manner about which he could do nothing. Odiva would immerse herself in a tank of water — wearing a thin diaphanous gold gown — and not come back up for air for two and a half minutes. During this time she would eat a banana underwater and then, in the words of one awestruck reviewer, "opens her pretty mouth to show that she has swallowed it right down."

"Can Muggsy McGraw do that? He *can't!*" remarked another hot-blooded and fascinated critic. "But also again, Odiva is a thousand times prettier and we are not a base-ball fan." Obviously this was the wet T-shirt exhibition of the day, something that made it very easy for red-blooded males to part with the dime or quarter admission charge.

At another time, when she wasn't doing her banana act, Odiva performed in a larger tank with a seal.

"You could easily tell Odiva from the seal," vaude-villian Joe Laurie recalled years later, "for she wore a one-piece bathing suit over a swell figure."

Yet for all the headlines and rave reviews grabbed by McGraw (including a curious one that said, "Odiva Does Things That Giants' Manager Wouldn't Dare Try") the act that was to grab the front-page headlines as well as the attention of the nation was the one that opened at Hammerstein's on October 29. And the press — both sporting and theatrical in New York—was quick to seize upon the fact that two Giants were actually competing at Broadway box offices.

Joe Kane had settled on Rube Marquard as the perfect athlete-performer to take the stage with his wife. A meeting had been arranged among Kane, Seeley, and Marquard on October 18, 1912, two days after the World Series had ended in Boston. Despite the fact that Marquard and Seeley had both heard of each other, they had never met.

At the meeting, Marquard could not take his eyes off Seeley. Rube, despite the nickname, was no rube at all. He had become a dapper sight around New York, given to expensive suits, good haircuts, fine manicures, and—if the presence of Annie Kent and Alice Joyce is any indication—the company of exceptionally attractive young women.

Marquard had also taken an apartment at the fashionable Hotel Endicott on East 28th Street. He even had a black manservant on call to assist him with personal affairs such as hailing cabs and picking up his clothes from the tailor. All of this seemed to be lost on Kane during the initial meeting. Joe was just trying to put on an act and serve as the ten-percenter.

So when Marquard had agreed to go back into vaudeville, Kane had hired a talented writer named Thomas Gray to prepare a comedy song-and-dance routine. Kane had also engaged composer W. Ray Walker to come up with some tunes.

Then, with his own unerring eye on the sporting public of New York, and the knowing eye of Willie Hammerstein upon the entire project, Kane had booked the act—inevitably—at Hammerstein's Victoria.

And he had given this new male-female "mixed act" a powerful but simple name with plenty of box office clout:

Marquard and Seeley. They would appear in a musical comedy skit titled, *Breaking the Record*; *or*, *Nineteen Straight.*

The "King of the Diamond," as Rube was now billed, and the "Queen of Ragtime," as Blossom was now known, would perform with each other.

Finally, Rube and Blossom were ready to entertain the nation. And not just onstage.

9

———◆———

Capacity, says an old bromide among theatrical producers, is all a theater can do. Amend that to capacity plus standing room, plus whatever the fire inspectors can be paid to ignore, and that was what Hammerstein's Victoria would do when Marquard and Seeley headlined.

The teaming of Rube Marquard and Blossom Seeley, already near the heights of their respective professions, would prove to be simultaneously the best and worst idea Joe Kane ever had in his life. Best professionally. Worst personally. But in the interim, New York went crazy over the prospects of seeing Marquard and Seeley live on stage together.

It must be remembered that the era before World War I, in addition to being somewhat mean-spirited, was also a very intimate time. The opportunity to see two stars endowed with disparate talents perform together was almost unique. Or at least that was the public perception that Willie Hammerstein carefully fostered. Tickets sold out quickly and scalpers—"sharps," as they were called—mysteriously cornered a huge supply of seats.

Marquard and Seeley opened on the twenty-ninth of October, 1912. At the Colonial, a few blocks down the Great White Way where McGraw was appearing, the SOLD OUT sign was prominent. So it was on the box office at Hammerstein's, too. And a crowd gathered around the Victoria Theater, just wanting to be where the excitement was. Inside the lobby, Willie Hammerstein sat in his usual crooked chair with his regular band of cronies. And the show — matinee and evening — went on.

A dumb act, as usual, opened the bill. This one featured a Mademoiselle Silverado, a pretty young acrobat who grabbed plenty of male attention as the audience moved to their seats.

She was followed by a slapstick quartet called the Monarch Comedy Four, and then a team of musicians named Conrad and Whitten, who played the piano and violin. Also on the bill was a monologist named Cliff Gordon, who shared a dressing room with Marquard beneath the stage. Gordon portrayed a "Dutch," meaning German orator, who did an act called "The German Senator." Gordon was something of an innovator, incorporating an excited rapid-fire delivery to portray a malaprop-prone German making a campaign speech for the U.S. Senate. It split up audiences time after time, including the one this evening at Hammerstein's

But there was no mistaking who would be the main event this night. The audience was noisy with anticipation when the turn came for Marquard & Seeley. And shortly after ten p.m. it was time for the headliners to come on stage.

Breaking the Record; or Nineteen Straight opened before a drop curtain that pictured the Polo Grounds. Seeley, to applause, appeared on stage first, wearing a plain but stylish white dress, the kind a lady of refinement might wear on the street.

Blossom had a short conversation with herself about going to the ball game. But when she uttered a question about who might be "pitching today," the audience grew so restless that they began to applaud. Rube's fans were present! A couple of thousand of them! Sensing the moment, Seeley cut short her lines, beckoned to her partner, and onto the stage strode Rube in a sharp blue business suit. A "tumultuous reception," according to the *New York Telegraph*, greeted the New York Giants star. When things quieted down, Marquard and Blossom exchanged pleasantries. Then Marquard continued through the clubhouse "door" — a space in the backdrop — and Seeley, confiding to the audience that she has just met the player who is her hero, broke into the type of song she delivered best, a syncopated ragtime number. This one had been specially concocted for this occasion, "The Marquard Glide."

> All you fans, All you fans
> Clap your hands, Clap your hands
> When you hear the tune
> That I'm goin' to croon,
> For it's there, It's a bear
> Right from the home plate;
> Gee, boys but it's great!

Here she goes,
On your toes!

(CHORUS:)

We'll do that Marquard Glide,
Yes, that Marquard Glide,
Matty, Meyers and McGraw,
Murray, Snodgrass and Devore,
Herzog, too! Flitch and Doyle,
Make that band of music toil
Oh, that Marquard Glide,
Oh, that Marquard Glide!

He's going down to second,
watch him slide!
He's king of the pitcher's box
Stood up through all the knocks,
Had it on those Red Sox,
You can bet all your rocks on
Reuben! Reuben!
He's some pitcher,
So we'll all do that Marquard Glide,
All do that Marquard Glide,
All do that Marquard Glide!

There was even a second verse.

Take your place, Take your place,

On your base, on your base,
Just when you hear that band
Don't it sound just grand!
Hear them shout,
Hit it out,
It makes a big score,
It makes you want more
Feel the sway,
Come this way.

And then the chorus repeated.

Heavy applause followed.

The scene was quickly changed via a second back-drop. Magically, the action moved within the Polo Grounds. Visible through a transparent window, Marquard was then in a Giants uniform, pitching the final inning of his nineteenth straight win.

On opening night, as this "story line" unfurled, Rube dropped one of the balls. It bounced, looking suspiciously like a tennis ball, much to the amusement of the audience.

Then the original curtain came down again, putting the lady back outside the ballpark. Seeley waited for her baseball hero much like a schoolgirl would. Marquard emerged in street clothes again. Seeley congratulated him on his record-breaking streak. Then Marquard and Seeley pulled up a couple of chairs that just happened to be on the edge of the stage, sat down hand in hand, and sang another Gray-Levi number titled, "Baseball."

First they sang it as a duet. Then Seeley rose and glided off the stage, leaving Marquard to entertain the cavernous Hammerstein's Victoria Theater by himself. And entertain, he did, standing and doing three stanzas of "Baseball" as a solo.

First the audience laughed along with Marquard, who seemed to take an I-may-not-be-good-but-I-got-a-lot-of-nerve approach. But then they roared with approval.

On being compelled to sing the chorus a final time, he teased his own fans. "It's your own fault. You've brought this on yourselves! I'll sing it once more!"

Heavy applause followed again. Seeley returned to the stage. Her white street dress was gone and she was now resplendent in a pink and blue gown. She picked up the tune and did her own rendition—polished and sharp enough to have the audience clapping and stomping in rhythm with her. She was good enough to dazzle, but in no way showed up her partner.

As she sang and danced, Rube dashed offstage. Seeley segued into a third song, "Those Ragtime Melodies," which soothed the audience and also allowed Rube to hit the wardrobe department. And then came the smash finale of the evening.

Following an astonishingly quick change, Rube reappeared. The ooh's and aaah's from the audience were even audible outside the theater. Rube was completely redone in black top hat and tails.

"Resplendent!" bellowed the *New York Review* the next morning.

"The big fellow looked ridiculously like a Shubert chorus man in formal evening clothes," raved *Variety*. "Rube in his claw hammer is a revelation! He has the height to carry the clothes and he actually wears them as if they were painless."

Marquard took Seeley's hand and the two hotfooted it for a brilliant dance number, something they apparently invented and called a "Gasotzky." The latter was a quick-tempoed rag dance — the type of two-step that Seeley had brought with her to New York from California. Seeley led all the way, but all eyes must have been on Rube, for the audience and critics were euphoric over the way he maintained the hectic hoofing.

"Rube brought down the house!" *Billboard* would thunder the following afternoon.

"The spectacle of the lengthy Rube dancing around the stage with the diminutive Miss Seeley is a wondrous sight and supplied a whirlwind finish!" reported Robert Speare in the *New York Telegraph* the next day. "The enthusiastic audience clapped for more and again the big pitcher threw his admirers into side-splitting laughter with his (encore) rendition of 'The Gasotzky Dance.'"

The *New York Herald* concurred as well.

"As Rube Marquard has appeared on the vaudeville stage before," wrote their critic, "audiences at Hammerstein's yesterday and last night were expecting big things of him. . . . And Rube rose to the occasion!"

The show stopped cold when the twenty-four-minute skit concluded. A thunderous ovation erupted, Marquard fans standing elbow to elbow with Seeley fans. Three encores were necessary and even the jaded Willie Hammerstein and his coterie of pals rose from their chairs in the lobby and wandered to the rear of the orchestra. There they marveled over how well things were going. The only way the crowd at the Victoria could eventually be calmed was for Marquard and Seeley to step out of character — to the extent that they had ever been in character, other than their own persona — and converse with the audience directly.

Seeley approached their fans first. "My son will now speak," she said, raising a hand.

The paying customers howled.

"Thank you, Mother, I shall," Rube said, continuing the joke.

Rube thanked the audience, but finally got flustered. He earned a sharp elbow in the ribs when he accidentally referred to his partner that night as "Miss Kent."

"How can you *think* of another woman when I'm around?" Blossom asked.

"I never will again," Rube answered, red-faced.

"You better believe you won't, darling," Blossom oozed. And the audience howled again.

A final round of applause led them offstage. The next morning the daily reviewers extolled the show and the teamwork. Words like "wondrous," "brilliant," "hilarious," and "has to be seen," filled the newspaper pages. Word also circulated up and down Broadway: Marquard and Seeley were not just a hit. They were a smash!

And of course they were even more than that.

Rube and Blossom were now headline stars. And they would continue to make the headlines — but not just for their performance onstage.

◆ ◆ ◆

Marquard and Seeley had first met on October 18. Their show opened ten days later. It was almost incomprehensible what had transpired in the meantime.

If Marquard's way with women had not been foremost in Kane's mind when he introduced the pitcher to his wife, the thought surely occurred to him soon afterward. Perhaps Joe Kane just didn't like the coziness with which Rube was rehearsing with Blossom, but by all observations, trouble began almost as soon as Marquard met Seeley. The wonder was that word of it didn't reach the New York newspapers for so long.

A week after rehearsals began, Kane confronted Blossom at their apartment at the Hotel Hermitage where they lived. At issue was Blossom's growing affection — later alleged as an emotional involvement — for Rube. Whatever Blossom's responses were to her husband's allegations, they hadn't washed well with him. Several more violent arguments erupted at home. Seeley would later allege that her husband beat her on these occasions. He was also, she said, in the habit of throwing things at her — a heavy clock and a lead mirror were cited as two items in particular. Kane never denied any of these charges.

Then, in the final and most violent of these domestic disputes, Kane assaulted Blossom with his fists, tore the clothing she was wearing, and then drew a pistol, threatening to kill her. Blossom fled her apartment and went to stay with her mother. The next day, she took a hack across town to the Endicott where Marquard was staying and — in terms of the hotel's ledger, at least — checked into a separate room.

Two days after that, Kane's jealous fury had moved up another notch. He arrived at the Victoria Theater, looking for Rube and Blossom. He brandished the same pistol with which Blossom alleged he had previously threatened her. And now his complaint had escalated, also. Marquard had "stolen" his wife and "wrecked my home," Kane ranted, waving the weapon in the air. He then — in front of several witnesses — threatened to shoot Seeley and possibly Marquard onstage during a performance if he had the opportunity. A few of Willie Hammerstein's muscular pals arrived on the scene to unceremoniously show Joe to the doorway.

Somehow everybody who was a witness to these altercations managed to keep quiet until the show had opened. Then, on the same day as the opening performance, Seeley went to the Jefferson Market Court to obtain a writ to keep Kane from coming anywhere near the Victoria Theater. Before Magistrate Keyran O'Connor, Seeley detailed the physical violence she had endured at her husband's hands. Marquard accompanied her to the court and stood by her as she spoke.

"By the way," Rube also added to Magistrate O'Connor at the hearing. "Blossom also has a new manager."

"Who is that?" O'Connor asked.

"Mr. Marquard," said Rube.

Judge O'Connor granted a temporary writ to prohibit Kane from legally entering the Victoria — or, for that matter, to come anywhere near Seeley in New York State. The judge also issued a summons for Kane — answerable within twenty-four hours—to reply to the charges against him.

Reporters were quick to note that on the same day that Marquard and Seeley were opening at Hammerstein's they were in court. Within hours the story was finally up and down Broadway. Within another day it was in the newspapers.

Several journals even reported the business angles of the Kane-Seeley rift. Kane, after all, was Blossom's agent as well as her husband. As the marriage neared the terminal stage, Blossom apparently offered to buy her "release" from Kane for $500. Obviously, Joe didn't take a first offer from anyone—even Blossom—and asked for $1,500 plus $60 per week while the Marquard and Seeley act worked. (By contract, Kane was due $100 per week for as long as Marquard and Seeley were performing.) On its own, ignoring other problems between Kane and Seeley, Joe's demand was not entirely unreasonable. Blossom, however, rejected it, most likely with Marquard's urging.

Reporters huddled around Rube that evening before the opening night performance. First they asked Seeley for her spin on the day's events. Her response was only two words, but politer than other two-word responses sometimes given to reporters.

"Ask Marquard," she said.

One of the questions that arose was why Seeley had gone to court to settle her differences with her husband. This was a time when such differences were often settled privately, or sometimes not at all.

"It was *my* idea that Blossom should go see the judge,"

Marquard said just minutes before their opening night bill took the stage at Hammerstein's Victoria. "What else could I do? Miss Seeley came to the theater with bruises on her face and I could not see her treated that way. I heard her husband had been making all kinds of threats — some of them as to what he would do with *me*. First I advised Miss Seeley to have orders given not to admit Kane to the theater under any conditions. Then I advised her to get a summons for him. That (going to court) seemed to be the best way to go. She said that she did not know how to go about it and I said I would go with her. That's about all there was to it."

Well, not completely all.

Marquard also recounted for the reporters how Seeley had returned to the Hermitage to pick up her wardrobe trunks. When she claimed them, someone had broken into them and slashed all her dresses. Rube, without proof but with a pretty good hunch, claimed Kane had been the culprit.

The inquiring minds of the day would certainly be eager to know about this, and the tabloid or "yellow" press was all over the story. But the "respectable" press carried it, too. Even the staid *New York Times* kept its readers apprised of the latest events in the Kane-Seeley-Marquard triangle. The difference in headlines, nonetheless, was noteworthy.

SAYS MARQUARD STOLE HIS ACTRESS-BRIDE

trumpeted one journal, while

RUBE MARQUARD IN COURT

was the headline in the *New York Times.*

In some papers, the account of the court action ran on the same page as the opening night reviews of Marquard and Seeley's *Nineteen Straight.* In other journals, the two stories were cross referenced.

As is frequently the case with Broadway business, however, *Variety* had the most memorable accounting of the events.

MARQUARD & SEELEY VS. KANE

ran their headline. Then their story, blending just the right show biz and baseball metaphors:

> It looks as though Rube Marquard is out for another record. He and Blossom Seeley form the headline battery at Hammerstein's this week. They appear to have Joe Kane on the bench. Joe seems to have had a low batting average lately, and he wasn't doing too well in the field, as Blossom hauled him into court Tuesday. She claimed Joe had made a balk by flourishing a revolver around the home grounds. The umpire on the bench issued a summons, and the newspaper boys present noted that the great left-hander occupied all the space on the coaching line . . . .

At the theater, Blossom has the star dressing room. Marquard is next door with Cliff Gordon. Joe Kane, still Miss Seeley's husband, finds himself barred from the Hammerstein diamond. They are afraid he might break up the game if allowed in the gate.

Kane answered his summons the next day in front of a crowded courtroom. Legally, however, Kane never had to address the issue of the violence he was alleged to have inflicted upon his wife. Instead, Kane would enter into an agreement with Seeley. She would consent to withdraw the summons against her husband in exchange for a letter from Kane agreeing to a legal separation.

Kane, who stood silently throughout the October thirtieth proceeding, gave her that letter. The correspondence was read in court and Kane acknowledged his agreement to it. Then Magistrate O'Connor dismissed the original summons against Kane.

A grim-faced Kane immediately left the courtroom, walking past reporters without speaking. He had lost the opening skirmish with his wife and client. But he had not yet lost the war. Joe still had more than a few cards to play.

In terms of public prurience, the only other news story that came close to that of Marquard and Seeley in 1912 involved the President of the United States, William Howard Taft.

The three-hundred-twenty-pound chief executive had become stuck in a too-snug bathtub in a hotel in Portland, Oregon. Taft was safely extricated by the always-glad-to-help-a-stuck-President Portland Fire Department. Then Taft went on to lose the Presidency to Woodrow Wilson, finishing a distant third behind both Wilson and the Bull Moose candidacy of Theodore Roosevelt. The election was held during the first week of Marquard and Seeley's appearance at Hammerstein's, and one wonders whether either had time to vote.

10

◆

Following their triumph at Hammerstein's Victoria on Broadway, Marquard and Seeley enjoyed a week off from their vaudeville schedule. Attempting to escape reporters, they traveled to Atlantic City, New Jersey. There they registered at the Hotel Dunlop on the morning of Friday, November 8. And there — naively, for some reason — they thought they would find some relief from Joe Kane.

Joe, however, was thinking otherwise.

Kane had put a pair of detectives on Marquard and Seeley in New York. His private eyes already knew that the couple had gone to Atlantic City. Fearing that Marquard or Seeley might recognize his New York operatives, Kane employed a pair of professional dicks from Philadelphia, a dubious pair of rumpled turn-of-the-century gumshoes named W.K. Carter and George Kinzie.

Carter and Kinzie had prowled around Atlantic City and had found an interesting item in the register of the Dunlop Hotel.

The entry read, "Rube Marquard and wife."

In the days when the Mann Act was taken seriously — making it illegal to transport a woman across state lines for "immoral purposes" — this could have been enough to send Marquard to jail, *if* it could be proven that he was in the hotel under a fraudulent registration. (Sticklers will note that Marquard did not say *whose* wife he was with.) Similarly, if Kane's dicks could prove that Marquard was there with Mrs. Kane, Kane would have greatly strengthened any subsequent legal action he chose to take against Rube or Blossom.

It was then, in short, well worth Marquard and Seeley's efforts *not* to get caught in any hotel hanky-panky. And it was equally worthwhile of Kane's efforts to catch them in the full stride of their friskiness.

On the evening of November eighth, Marquard and Seeley emerged from one of the main elevators of the hotel, having descended from the Dunlop's "Parlor C," a lavish suite overlooking the Atlantic Ocean. Not only was Joe Kane hiding behind a newspaper in a corner of the lobby — the New York court order had enjoined him only from staying away from Blossom in New York State — but so were Kinzie and Carter. This would prove to be an evening of comedy, both high and low.

Marquard and Seeley took a hand-holding stroll on the city's famed boardwalk, apparently oblivious of the crude shadowing efforts behind them. Kane stayed far out of sight as Kinzie and Carter did the gumshoe routine.

Rube and Blossom went to Atlantic City's Apollo Theater where they caught the evening's vaudeville bill, something of a busman's holiday for the two entertainers. The two dicks stayed in the rear of the theater and kept an eye on Marquard and Seeley throughout the performance. Then they took up the trail again as Rube and Blossom came out of the Apollo and on a brisk, clear night took a rolling chair up the boardwalk to the Disleworth Cafe. There the couple stopped for a late supper, as Carter and Kinzie watched from a distance. Afterward, Rube and Blossom strolled back to the Dunlop, bringing their escorts — still apparently unnoticed — along with them.

Then Kinzie and Carter observed Rube and Blossom step into the hotel's elevator. The two detectives watched as the arrow above the elevator indicated a stop at the second floor. Apparently, both Rube and Blossom stepped out, as the elevator then returned to the lobby. By this time, Kane himself — the irate cuckolded husband — was in the lobby to oversee the proceedings. A few minutes later, the detectives took Kane upstairs.

Kinzie and Carter had managed to rent the room right next to Marquard's. The walls were conveniently and provocatively thin. Kane and his two detectives spent two hours sitting in the adjoining room with their ears pressed to the wall, listening to the chatting voices of Rube and Blossom. Meanwhile, Kane and his dicks then prepared to make their next move.

All things considered, two-thirty a.m. was eventually seen as just the right time. Exactly what the detectives felt was in progress in Rube's room was never exactly spelled out in the ensuing court papers, but one could imagine.

Kane and the detectives assembled outside the door

to Parlor C and apparently no longer could tolerate the sounds that emanated from within. Kane gave a nod. Kinzie rapped sharply at the door, announcing that he was a detective and that Marquard should open up.

A sudden silence ensued from within Parlor C.

Kane gave another nod and his two detectives began shouldering the door. The Dunlop Hotel, however, proved to be a solid edifice. The carpenters who had hung those doors had done a laudable job. The big oak portals wouldn't budge, at least not immediately.

"For five minutes we battered that door with our shoulders, all three of us," Kane would later tell eager reporters. "Finally, it gave way."

When the door finally lifted off its hinges, Kane pushed through the doorway first, hoping to catch his wife in *en flagrante*. But, if nothing else, the five minutes of battering had alerted the occupants of the room that something was up. When Kinzie and Carter bulled their way into the room after Kane, all three were met with an untidy room, but no human beings in view.

Not that the sight that greeted them was one that pleased Joe Kane.

"My wife's clothing hung across a chair," Kane recalled later. "And Marquard's clothes were across other pieces of furniture. Two suitcases, including one that I recognized as belonging to Mrs. Kane, were also nearby."

There were only so many possibilities as to where Blossom and Rube had gone. The detectives, being detectives, explored them quickly.

They went to a front window, and they saw nothing

other than a nice view of the Atlantic Ocean. Then they opened a closet and found—as they later insisted— Marquard hiding behind a pair of heavy winter coats. He was wearing little more than an embarrassed and angry expression. The detectives claimed that they pulled him out of the closet.

Joe Kane had the privilege of locating his wife, at least according to his account. He looked under the bed and found Blossom "huddled far back against the wall," as he told the *New York Telegraph* the next day, and wearing "the flimsiest of negligees." He reached under the bed and—as she struggled indignantly—yanked her out.

There they then stood, the five of them, the air alive with insult and allegation. Kinzie was searching his jacket pocket for a summons to serve upon Marquard, while Carter made noises about calling the Atlantic City police to have Marquard arrested. Blossom broke loose long enough to find a robe.

Enter Bob Delaney, the hotel manager, who had been drawn by the commotion and was less than happy about the oak door that was now lying on the floor.

Delaney demanded an explanation.

Kane was all too pleased to give him one.

Delaney eyed the detectives and his guests and—as a veteran hotel manager—immediately had a pretty good idea what was going on. He also had a pretty good idea how the Dunlop Hotel's name might look in the newspapers and on the police blotters. The manager also knew who was a paying client of the hotel and who wasn't, which also probably influenced his eventual sympathies.

A moment later, Delaney was joined by the night clerk, a man named Frank Bowman, who had also been drawn upstairs by the noisy break-in.

"The very least you might do," Delaney finally said to Kane, Kinzie, and Carter, "is withdraw for a moment while my guests get dressed."

Kane protested.

Delaney repeated the request, and added some utterances about his own detectives who would soon be on the scene. Delaney also gave a conspiratorial nod to Bowman, the night clerk, who quickly went downstairs. Eventually, Marquard mumbled something about coming downstairs in a few minutes. Grudgingly, Kane, Kinzie, and Carter finally stepped from Parlor C, leaving Delaney in the hallway with Kane and the two detectives.

Delaney immediately launched into a short discussion of how "unwise" it would be for everyone if the police were called. Kane was not in much of a mood to listen. Moments later the night clerk Bowman reappeared on the second floor. Delaney, meanwhile, entreated Kane, Kinzie, and Carter to go downstairs and wait in the lobby for Marquard and Seeley.

Grudgingly again, Kane led his entourage downstairs, but once there, Detective Kinzie phoned Atlantic City police and asked for an arrest to be made.

In the meantime, acting on the instructions of his manager, night clerk Bowman was working overtime. He raced back upstairs to Parlor C. Marquard, expecting to see Kane's gumshoes again, was relieved to see the night clerk and allowed Bowman to talk. Bowman explained that the police were very probably on their way.

"There is, however," Bowman explained, "one solution."

Marquard and Seeley were anxious to hear what it was.

"Get dressed," said Bowman, "and get out of here. Compliments of Mr. Delaney."

Marquard and Seeley threw on a few articles of clothing. Bowman then led them to a window at the end of a second-floor hallway. The window led to an exterior iron fire escape. Hotel management had already arranged for a taxi, presumably one from an understanding hack company that was used to picking up half-dressed couples fleeing hotels through the second-story rear exit.

Marquard went onto the fire escape first, then held out a hand for Seeley. Then Rube and Blossom hurried down the clanking metal steps. Moments later they were on the ground near a dusty incinerator at the rear of the hotel.

The cab cranked its engine. Detective Kinzie, hearing a motor vehicle arrive, stop, and then turn over at such an unusual hour, immediately sensed something amiss. He glared out a rear window of the hotel's lobby, only to have his eyes go wide when he saw Marquard and Seeley—barely dressed beneath winter coats—hurrying into a taxi.

"They're getting away!" Kinzie bellowed.

And the alarm was out. Kane, Kinzie, and Carter raced through the lobby, out the front door and around to the back of the hotel, only to glimpse a view of the taillights of the taxi as it pulled away.

It took Kane and his erstwhile sleuths several minutes to hail another cab. One of the detectives—correctly—guessed that Marquard and Seeley had probably fled to the railroad station. But when Kane and his gumshoes arrived at the depot, the night train to Philadelphia was just leaving. The ticket agent confirmed that a disheveled man and woman matching the description of Marquard and Seeley had hopped aboard practically as the train was moving out.

Once again, Kane found himself partially victorious and partially foiled. He had caught his wife in a hotel room with Marquard, but lacked an arrest. Kane and his detectives departed immediately for Philadelphia on the next train but the trail of the lovers was hours cold by the time they arrived. Wherever Marquard and Seeley had gone to in William Penn's Sleepy City, they had this time registered under completely fictitious names.

In person, they were nowhere to be found.

In the newspapers two days later, however, they were everywhere.

It was not enough that Joe and Blossom's messy separation coincided with Marquard and Seeley's opening night at Hammerstein's. For a public that was salivating with curiosity about big-time stars, here were the ingredients for a big time scandal. It was difficult to find a major city newspaper that didn't give prominent space to the story.

PITCHER TRAPPED IN ROOM WITH ACTRESS

howled the *Philadelphia Inquirer*.

TAKES FIRE ESCAPE WHEN HUSBAND
ALLOWS TIME TO DRESS

WITH "BLOSSOM SEELEY" HE FLEES FROM
ATLANTIC CITY TO AVOID ARREST.

ran the subtitles.

Then there was barely a detail missing, including extensive quotes from the wronged husband. In fact, most of the press had a ball with the story.

MARQUARD FLEEING!
BLOSSOM WITH HIM

screamed the *New York American*.

RUBE TRIES FOR SPEED RECORD
AFTER MISS SEELEY'S SPOUSE
RAIDS ATLANTIC CITY HOTEL

And on it went.

KANE WOULD PUT BLOSSOM
AND RUBE IN JAIL

bellowed the *New York Review*.

The *Review*'s account of the story followed most others, paying special attention to the details of the fire escape, the warrant, and what was coyly termed, "a serious offense," which readers were on their own to conclude was both adultery and a violation of the Mann Act.

Once again, even the sane and sober *New York Times* couldn't lay off this story, though their reporter toned things down a bit so as not to have Park Avenue matrons collapsing in shock over their breakfasts on Sunday, November 10.

KANE PURSUING MARQUARD

ran the headline. And after bringing readers up to date with a few paragraphs of backstory, the *Times* then offered this delicate — if slightly inaccurate — summary account.

> It was 2 o'clock this morning when Kane finally pounced on one of the doors in the hotel and broke his way in, but by that time the two occupants had gone out walking. They left at a brisk athletic pace by way of the fire escape, and now Kane is looking for the wonderful Rube with a warrant charging him, for one thing, with alienating his Blossom's affections.

Somewhere back in New York, in between stints playing to packed houses at the Colonial, McGraw had to be reading about all of this — and seething.

Rube and Blossom eventually drifted back to Manhattan, and not so secretly took up residence again at the Endicott. They were a front-page story now on the scandal sheets, and first-class gossip in both the sports world and on Broadway. The accounts of their flight from the Dunlop Hotel in Atlantic City had even drifted into the "respectable" press around the country, papers which didn't normally run stories about who had been caught with whom in whose bedroom.

But if they were the cynosure of public attention, they were never far from Joe Kane's thoughts, either.

Kane had been legally enjoined from stalking his wife or even coming close to her. But that didn't mean he didn't have a few weapons, even in New York State. From Kane's point of view, remaining the cuckolded husband — albeit an abusive one who had probably brought much of the cuckoldry upon himself — was a no-win situation. He might as well get something out of it.

Who better to employ when one wishes to reverse one's legal fortunes than a lawyer?

From some of his more questionable dealings on Broadway, Kane had just the mouthpiece, a legal eaglet named Nicholas Selvaggi. Selvaggi toiled at a firm called Schnauer and Morris, located at 320 Broadway. Selvaggi would have made a dandy ambulance chaser had he not been so busy chasing prominent people with writs.

Two days after returning to New York via Philadelphia, and one week following the spectacular fire escape extravaganza in Atlantic City, Rube and the still-Mrs. Kane were looking over the menus one midnight at a choice table at the Folies Bergere Restaurant. A man approached their table and engaged them in friendly conversation.

"You're Rube Marquard, the winner of nineteen straight wins for the Giants, aren't you?" asked the stranger.

Rube looked the man up and down and admitted that he was. The man then turned to Blossom.

"And you're Blossom Seeley. The Queen of Ragtime?"

Blossom looked at the man long and hard, her dark eyes alive with suspicion, then admitted that's who she was. The man had a folded sheet of paper in his hands and seemed to be working up the nerve to ask for an autograph.

"I am, darling," Blossom finally said. Then she took a final closer look at their visitor. Her expression changed.

"Be careful, Richard," she was heard to say. (She always called Marquard, "Richard." Never "Rube.") "This man's a friend of Joe's!"

He was. But the man did indeed wish a signature. Marquard's. The problem was, however, that he was not just an autograph hound. He was Kane's lawyer Selvaggi, in his evening role as a process server. And he was serving a summons on Rube.

Kane had now filed an alienation of affection suit against Marquard, claiming that the ballplayer "has robbed me of my wife's love and affections by attentions, numerous gifts, and by abusing, slandering, and belittling me in the presence of Blossom Cahane."

The suit also alleged that Marquard had "wickedly, willfully, and maliciously" exerted an influence over the mind and disposition of Joe Kane's actress wife. The suit further charged that the author of nineteen straight wins had notched yet another series of victories when he had "kissed Mrs. Cahane in the presence of several people at a tavern in Central Park," registered with her "as man and wife" at various hotels, and was currently "detaining her for nonprofessional reasons" at the Hotel Endicott. The damages Kane sought from the pitcher made a nice round number.

Twenty-five thousand dollars' worth of damages.

So much for dinner.

Three days later, Kane struck again.

As Marquard and Seeley were out in public on a brisk November evening near the Endicott on East 28th Street, Attorney Schnauer of Schnauer and Morris himself appeared to serve Blossom. This time he bore papers in a suit for "absolute divorce from husband, Joseph Cahane." The suit named Marquard as corespondent and alleged repeated adultery at the nearby Endicott, at the Hotel Dunlop in Atlantic City, and at yet another cozy little love nest in Passaic, New Jersey.

The service of papers attracted a crowd. Apparently, less than cordial words were exchanged between Rube and Schnauer. Rube accepted the papers — not that he had an option — and quickly withdrew to the Endicott with Blossom.

One can only imagine what the lovers discussed that evening. But whatever discomfort or anxiety the two lawsuits caused, it didn't last. Rube quickly retained a starchy-collar law firm called Rifkind and Samuels, a high-powered Broadway operation, and didn't appear terribly upset in the days that followed.

Rube, in fact, suddenly began to sound like an expert on the psychology of love.

"As to alienating affections," Rube told a reporter on November 16, "I'm no alienist. Blossom never manifested any love or affection for her husband. Since there was no affection, I couldn't have alienated any."

"Joe and I," Seeley added carefully, "never lived together peaceably, happily, or harmoniously. We were never truly husband and wife in the way a man and woman should be."

"Nor did I ever exert any influence over Blossom of a wicked, willful, or malicious nature," Rube added.

Nonetheless, with the summonses served, now the two cases would have to wend their way through the legal system. Kane managed to stay away from Marquard and Seeley as they continued their triumphant appearances on Broadway, the box office buoyed enormously by all the publicity.

Proving again that there is no such thing as bad publicity, the notoriety that had descended upon their partnership had turned Marquard and Seeley into the hottest ticket in New York. Perhaps with an eye to paying his growing legal fees, Marquard had taken the first steps of cashing in.

First, he signed with the Keith organization to extend his vaudeville run for an impressive *twenty-two weeks*, including a national tour that would take him to California through late May—one full month into the 1913 baseball season.

And second, sending John McGraw an additional headache, Marquard voiced his salary demands for the following season.

Marquard wanted a cool $10,000 to take the field and pitch for the New York Giants in 1913.

In making such a demand, Marquard was asking for the same salary as Christy Mathewson. Ten grand was also five hundred dollars more than Ty Cobb would be paid by the Detroit club and $3,500 more than the noble Walter Johnson (who in his time referred to baseball as a form of financial "slavery") was paid by the parsimonious Washington Americans. (Johnson might have added that just *pitching* for Clark Griffith's Washington team was a form of slavery.) Putting things further in perspective, the Giants' first baseman, Fred Merkle, a regular starting player and one year older than Marquard, earned a mere $3,000 per season.

Ten thousand dollars a year.

"Ain't I worth it?" Marquard asked a reporter.

The reporter didn't answer. But somewhere across town both John McGraw and Harry Hemstead, the new owner of the Giants, had to be pouring themselves a row of stiff drinks. Here was the first hint that Rube, *the* outstanding pitcher in the National League for the past two years, might have something more interesting to do than play baseball.

11

———◆———

The initial hearing on the Kane-Seeley divorce proceeding was set for December 17, 1912 in the New York State Supreme Court. Reporters hung around the courtroom like a pack of flies throughout the testimony.

Blossom, perhaps reflecting Rube's outlook on this, seemed to adopt an "I should worry?" attitude toward the entire proceeding. Not only did she not show up at the hearing, or make any response to it, she did not even hire an attorney to look after her interests. Very obviously, she must have felt that the "worst" thing that could happen was also the best—she would be granted a divorce from Kane.

Rube and Blossom, for that matter, arranged to have bookings out of town while Kane was in court, sparing them the nuisance of an appearance and keeping the contentious New York press at bay. So while Joe made waves in court, Marquard and Seeley had their show on the road—literally—playing Indianapolis, Pittsburgh, and other points in the Midwest.

All of which did not mean that Marquard was out of the newspapers. His contract squabble with the Giants had quickly escalated, and subsequent negotiations were being played out primarily in the press.

"If McGraw doesn't show me a parchment with $10,000 written all over it," Marquard boasted, "I'll play out my full (twenty-two-week) vaudeville schedule. Who needs baseball when I can tour with Blossom?"

McGraw replied that Marquard was "turning into another Mike Donlin," which was not meant as a compliment, nor was it received as one.

"Mike would never have quit baseball if it hadn't been for Mabel Hite," the Giant manager insisted. "I'm afraid Rube's dumb enough to pull the same thing."

The "dumb enough" phrase apparently hit the hot button for Rube, who then alleged that his act with Blossom was not only *better* than Hite and Donlin, but it also sparkled much more brightly than "McGraw stuffed into his monkey suit telling baseball stories at the Colonial. Why, Mr. McGraw would be afraid to be on the same bill with us."

McGraw's answer to that sizzled with the unprintable.

Then, at a further point, after a show in Pittsburgh on December 13, reporters asked Marquard if he was married. He smiled.

"No," he answered. "But Blossom and I will be if she gets a divorce. That fellow Kane has caused me a lot of trouble, and now he's suing Miss Seeley for divorce and me for $25,000. I hope he wins the first one." There was no mention of any troubles Rube may have created for Joe. But "that fellow Kane," as Marquard termed him, was in New York at that very hour, trying to win both of his lawsuits.

The hearing in the New York court was a juicy rehash of the events of Atlantic City on November 8. The events, obviously, were crucial to Kane's suit for divorce against his wife. Adultery—in addition to making fine newspaper headlines—was the only grounds for divorce in the Empire State. The modern concept of "no fault" divorce—which might have worked just fine in this case—was not an option in 1913.

Kane took the stand first, alleging again how Marquard had run off with his wife and how he, the self-proclaimed long-suffering spouse, had traced the adulterous couple to Atlantic City, only to break into their room and be shocked—*shocked!*—at what he had found. And this in lack of appreciation for having made his wife a star, Kane complained.

"And it was not even a professional matter that was keeping them together in that room," Kane intoned suggestively to the court.

Detectives Kinzie and Carter, relishing their moment in the national spotlight, next gave a gleeful account of events as they remembered them, corroborating Kane's testimony.

Summonses were issued for two other reluctant witnesses from that hot spot of immorality, the Hotel Dunlop in Atlantic City—hotel manager Bob Delaney and night clerk Frank Bowman. Delaney insisted that he was too "ill" to travel to New York to testify. And Bowman apparently suffered from a selective form of amnesia. Eventually, however, both responded to summonses issued and appeared in court, though their testimony was interrupted by the Christmas court holiday. The hearing did not convene again until January 1913.

Bowman testified first and obviously was not enjoying his trip to New York. He did everything he could, short of perjury, to protect the Giants' pitcher, even referring to Marquard's lady guest as "Mrs. Marquard," as suggested by the hotel register.

As for specific details of the two-thirty a.m. raid, Bowman's memory proved even foggier.

Kane, however, led the cross-examination, bleeding details out of a highly embarrassed night clerk.

"What was Mr. Marquard's lady guest wearing?" Kane asked.

Bowman blushed and explained that the woman hadn't had much on other than "a sheer nightdress that was cut very low at the neck."

Reporters enthusiastically jotted that one down for the next morning's early editions. Bowman also conceded that the woman he took to be "Mrs. Marquard" certainly bore a remarkable resemblance to the most recent Mrs. Kane, Blossom Seeley. Kane had Blossom's publicity stills in court for the convenience of his witnesses as well as reporters.

As to how the couple registered as "Rube Marquard and wife" happened to elude the Atlantic City vice squad that night, Bowman — sweating profusely by this time —

at first said that they had slipped away "in an unaccountable manner."

When Kane first pressed this point, Bowman held firm to his selective amnesia. But under relentless prodding from Kane, the memory of Bowman improved.

Kane stated that he, Kane, had a miraculous aptitude at recognizing footprints. He could, he said, identify his wife's shoe and the footprint of his wife anywhere.

"I found Blossom's footprint in the dust on the ground behind the hotel," he stated. "Right near the incinerator. I also found the heel of her shoe."

Kane brandished this in court. When it was shown to the night clerk, and identified as belonging to the woman who had escaped with Marquard, Bowman made a concession.

"The couple *might* have escaped by the rear fire entrance," Bowman said.

Kane and his attorney were elated. At that moment, the Hotel Dunlop had the most famous rear fire escape in the United States, and the night clerk was about the only person in the country who expressed any doubts over whether Rube and Blossom had climbed down it on the early morning of November ninth.

Kane's team had feared they might not be able to legally identify as Blossom the woman with Marquard. Failing that, they would not have enough corroborated evidence in the divorce hearing to win. And winning the divorce hearing was the first step to winning the alienation of affection suit. But now, as Kane finished pressing Bowman, that identification seemed assured.

The hearing concluded on January 15, 1913. Rube and Blossom remained far away from Manhattan and the courtroom. In the late afternoon on the final day of hearing, Justice Paul Hendrick asked Kane if he had "voluntarily lived with Miss Seeley since you discovered her preference for Mr. Marquard."

For some reason, Kane seemed to hesitate with his answer. Then he spoke. "No, I have not," he said.

An hour later, Justice Hendrick granted Joe Kane a decree of divorce from his wife. News reached Marquard and Seeley the next morning. It was their turn to share in the elation.

The Orpheum Theater in San Francisco was one of the top houses in Seeley's native city, if not *the* top. Its owners grandly called it, "The safest and most magnificent theater in America," which was a nice way of saying that it was new, top quality in terms of entertainment, and was not a firetrap, as so many wooden theaters were. It was at the Orpheum that Marquard and Seeley, who were continuing their national tour, were booked in March 1913.

Admission to a matinee at the Orpheum was a dime, a quarter, or fifty cents, depending how close a viewer wished to be to the stage. At night a patron could still sit up in the nosebleed section for a dime, but prices for other locations were scaled all the way up to one dollar for the high rollers who wished to sit down front in a box seat.

There were two shows every day — matinee and evening, the former at 2:15 p.m., the latter at 8:15. This included Sunday, which was a big day in terms of admissions. All that added up to fourteen shows a week for any performer booked at the Orpheum, with no break, no understudies, no days off. And performers would scratch one another's eyes out for a chance to play the house.

The show at the Orpheum was a typical top quality card of the day. A paying customer could get a lot for his ten pennies, notwithstanding the remote possibility of nasal hemmorhage. Twice daily, the house musicians, who were billed as "E.M. Rosner's Augmented Hungarian Orchestra" started things off with a rousing march entitled "That Old Girl of Mine" to open the eyes of the patrons. The music also served as an overture to the show. It also helped get the tardy to their seats before the more visual and audible acts came onstage.

Second on the bill was an act called Apdale's Zoological Circus, which featured four bears, eight dogs, three monkeys, and — with a mildly incongruous touch — one ant eater. One of Apdale's specialties — if it can be called that — was a chariot race, with dogs made up as horses and monkeys as the drivers. Another "dumb" act, in other words, perhaps in more ways than one.

Apdale's was followed by a "mixed" comedy team, Diamond & Brennan, Diamond being a man named James, Brennan being a woman named Sibyl. Together they formed — in case you didn't notice — an overtly "Jew and Irish" act. Their skit was called *Niftynonsense.*

Then came one of the main events, a "musical pantomime" play called *Puss in Boots*, which was a short laughfest in four scenes, headlined by Will J. Kennedy, a well-known vaudevillian of the day. If a potential viewer wished to get the drift of this piece and assess how seriously it was meant to be taken, he needed only to know that "Wanda Mann, the Village spinster," was played by a male actor named Fred Wilson.

Once the curtain came down on *Puss in Boots*, the augmented Hungarians in the orchestra pit took over again, playing a "dance parisienne" and a waltz, thus also allowing a set change.

A short comedy followed, four characters, one act, entitled "The Late Mr. Allen." It was coauthored by Bozeman Bugler, the New York sportswriter.

Then on came another headliner, Eddy Howard, who had recently left a popular comedy duo called Howard and North. Here was an interesting point. Two-man comedy teams had undergone a transformation in the last ten years. Formerly, both partners had dressed up in funny clothing—a badly fitting suit, mismatching shoes, a fake nose, a ridiculous hat, and so on. Now only the comic would dress that way, while the straight man would wear "street clothes," if a slick suit, two-toned button shoes, and a gray derby could be called street clothes. This way, promoters discovered, the audiences were better primed as to who was giving the setup lines and who was delivering the jokes.

These two-man teams had also dispensed with the "By the way, what happened to you on the way to the theater?" type of gag and now did set comedy pieces. Of this category, the enduringly famous routine by Abbott

& Costello, *Who's On First*, was perhaps the all-time greatest. Tonight in San Francisco, Howard had jettisoned
North in favor of Bert Snow, but he did an old Howard
and North routine called *Those Were The Happy Days*.

Then came Marquard and Seeley, having brought their
act — and their notoriety — all the way from New York.
They were two acts before the close, the featured spot in
almost any bill. They were followed by a pair of acrobats
named Wotpurt and Paulan, who entertained with a series of catapulting exercises, and a short motion picture,
which was all the rage now as a way to close a show.

It was not unusual for vaudeville audiences to start
fumbling for the exits after the last headline act. So the
position of the new "novelty" motion pictures at the end
was an attempt to keep audiences in their seats. Only
the most farsighted promoters — and there were a few —
could see that motion pictures, now creeping in at the
end of daily bills, would eventually replace their entire
industry.

After the film, the orchestra pit struck up an exit
march called "When I Join My Honey Down in Jacksonville," E.M. Rosner again conducting. The exit march was
the hint for the audience to beat it out into the night.

Marquard and Seeley wowed the opening night critics in San Francisco and subsequently played to appreciative houses. Meanwhile, the lovers needed to make a
decision on how to further arrange their personal and
professional relationships.

Blossom was pregnant.

◆◆◆

Wednesday, March 12, 1913, would turn out to be a very important day for both Rube and Blossom, but particularly for Rube.

In the morning, Rube and Blossom emerged from their quarters for a short walk in downtown San Francisco. They went to a town clerk and took out a marriage license, upon which Marquard gave his name as Richard LeMarquis, and, in a bizarre touch that would have sent her most recent husband through the ceiling, Blossom gave her name as Katherine Kane.

Returning to the hotel, they were recognized on the street by several fans and admirers, and stopped to sign autographs. After lunch, they hurried to the Orpheum Theater for their matinee. No sooner was their afternoon performance over — they were eighth on a bill that featured ten acts, don't forget — they continued to the nearby German Evangelical Lutheran Church, and at a four o'clock service Marquard and Seeley were married.

There were two theatrical friends in attendance, plus a phalanx of reporters outside the parsonage where the service was held. Later they were joined in an informal party with a handful of Marquard's baseball friends, though most of his teammates were already at spring training in Texas.

In the evening, one of the honeymooners had another piece of business.

McGraw had sent one of his top scouts, "Sinister Dick" Kinsella, west to sign Marquard. Men with the nickname of "Sinister" tend to get results.

Kinsella placed a new contract before Rube. Marquard

finally signed for a substantial increase in salary, enough to get Marquard to end his long and noisy holdout.

Reporters badgered Kinsella for the terms of the contract, but Kinsella remained tight-lipped. It was believed to be short of the ten thousand dollars per year for which Rube had been yammering, but not by much. Years later, in a moment of retrospective candor, Marquard pegged the figure at $8,500.

"McGraw commissioned me to corral Rube and I did," Sinister Dick said, puffing on a cigar. "I used my own judgment in drawing up the contract, but I know it will stand." In other words, Kinsella had inked Marquard for a figure within the range McGraw had dictated.

The contract specifically called upon Marquard to quit his theatrical work and report to Marlin, Texas, for spring training. And finally, Blossom agreed to go with him. But meanwhile, the newlyweds had to quickly duck back into the Orpheum where they hoofed and sang and otherwise emoted in yet another performance of "Breaking the Record."

How much the pregnancy dictated their plans can only be imagined. And certainly it precipitated the wedding. But Blossom, four months' pregnant on her second wedding day (in a year and a half) was obviously not looking to stay on tour—particularly without her husband—during the next few months. So at least some matters had been settled. For the foreseeable future, Blossom would be a baseball wife.

There remained, of course, one large piece of unfinished business. Blossom may have divorced Joe Kane, but her noisy ex-spouse still had warrants out for the love-birds in several states. The divorce may have been settled, but there was the matter of the civil action. In fact, Kane had doubled the stakes, claiming that Blossom's affections were now worth fifty grand.

"(Kane is still) suing Marquard for $50,000 for the alienation of his wife's affections," the *Morning Telegraph* reminded readers within the article covering Rube and Blossom's wedding day.

"Will he get it?" mused the writer of the article. "Maybe. Maybe not." It was as good a guess as anyone had as to the outcome of Kane's legal complaint. And it was also a reminder that Kane and his team of lawyers and private gumshoes would be waiting as soon as Mr. and Mrs. Marquard ventured back east.

Rube, however, now a twenty-three-year-old newly-wed, could not miss the opportunity to clutch — literally — one final bit of publicity while in San Francisco.

A few years earlier Washington Senators catcher Gabby Street had caught a baseball thrown to him off the summit of the Washington Monument. A few years later, Wilbert Robinson would attempt to catch a baseball tossed from a low-flying airplane. Robinson's baseball eventually turned out to be a grapefruit, courtesy of that world-class prankster, Casey Stengel. Such stunts were always good for drawing a crowd, creating publicity, getting one's picture in the papers, and showing what a swell athlete one was, all at the same time.

So before leaving the City by the Bay for Marlin Springs, Marquard arranged his own stunt. A baseball was thrown to him from the tenth floor of the Call Building.

Rube, risking a broken wrist, caught the ball on the fly with his newly signed pitching hands.

"Good stuff!" proclaimed one of the San Francisco papers the next day.

The picture appeared in many newspapers across the country. When John McGraw saw it in Texas, however, his comment was not quite the same as the journalist's in California. Nor—like many quotes from McGraw—could it have appeared in print.

12

---◆---

After the events of the off-season, the 1913 baseball season seemed almost anticlimactic.

Marquard reported late to the Giants, newly married and his contract squabble with McGraw settled. Seeley accompanied him to Texas and then to New York where the new bride and groom took up a new residence together at 549 Riverside Drive.

With that settled—or as close to being settled as it could be—Rube and Blossom settled in for life as a celebrity two-career husband-and-wife team in New York. This wasn't as easy as it might have been for most couples: Marquard was still badgered by some of the unfriendly press, which had the notion that his behavior had not been quite as exemplary as a baseball hero's should be. Additionally, Kane's lawyers continued to hound him via the alienation of affection suit, which was still unsettled. Nor were the Marquards the only people at 549 Riverside Drive with legal problems.

One of Seeley's fur coats disappeared from their apartment, as did a set of silver. Systematically, several other apartments in the building were also burglarized. When one resident spotted some of his stolen possessions in a nearby pawn shop, city detectives got busy with the case, eventually arresting — as the *New York American* so indelicately put it — "William Keene, twenty-seven, of ebony hue, who had worked as an elevator operator in the building."

When the police raided Keene's apartment in Harlem, they found seventy-five similar pawn tickets, and, surprise of surprises, used all of them to locate stolen property. The Marquards recovered some of their property, as did seven other residents of 549 Riverside. Keene drew a stern lecture from Judge Michael Foster of the Manhattan Court of General Sessions, plus a one-year state-sponsored vacation in Elmira Reformatory, as it was then known.

Then there was Blossom's career. And condition. Approximately four months' pregnant at the time of their marriage, she no longer exactly fit the visual image of the saucy-yet innocent (sort of) soubrettes that she had portrayed onstage. In keeping with the custom of the day, she kept her public appearances to a minimum. A healthy son was born in August of that year.

As if he needed it, Rube had a further distraction during the season — this one medical. Rube suffered for a significant part of the season from a brutal case of tonsillitis, which was no small problem in the days before antibiotics and modern surgical procedures. In retrospect, it is difficult to tell which was more miraculous — the fact that Rube was able to keep his mind on baseball at all, or that he would again manage to turn in a great season on the mound, his third in a row.

Ever mindful of the need for some *positive* publicity from time to time—as opposed to the type of publicity the club had normally received recently—McGraw signed the part-American Indian Jim Thorpe to a $5,000 contract to play baseball for the New York Giants in 1913. In the Stockholm Olympics the previous summer, Thorpe had won the pentathlon and decathlon competitions and had informally been crowned by King Gustav V of Sweden as "the greatest athlete in the world."

The greatest athlete in the world had blinding speed and a wonderfully strong throwing arm—thus accounting for his triumphs at sprinting and javelin and discus throwing. Hitting a curve ball proved more vexing, however, and the signing began to look more and more like a publicity stunt as Thorpe spent the first of six frustrating summers in the National League, mostly riding the bench.

"I felt like a sitting hen, not a ballplayer," Thorpe once said. Ironically, and quite unfairly, Thorpe's earlier involvement in baseball—the same sport that so frustrated him after the Olympics—was what eventually caused his medals to be revoked. He had played two summers of semipro baseball in Pennsylvania before the world games.

An infielder named Eddie Grant joined the Giants that year, too. Harvard-educated, clean living, and well spoken, Grant was an above-average ballplayer but an outstanding human being. Many years later, however, he would suffer an even more tragic fate than Thorpe. Grant was the only active major league ball player to die in World War I, perishing before German artillery in the Verdun Forest in 1918. A plaque to his memory would be erected near the centerfield clubhouse of the Polo Grounds in 1919 and would remain there till the Giants deserted the park in September 1957. And on the subject of ballparks, 1913 also saw the opening of Ebbets Field in Brooklyn, a cozy ball yard that rose in a smelly fetid shantytown and eventually hosted 32,000 fans, many legends, and enough zaniness to last sportswriters for the rest of the twentieth century.

Three events on opening day set the tone at the Brooklyn club's new home. The official gatekeeper, in charge of unlocking the park, forgot the key. The local sportswriters looked for the press box and discovered that there was none. And when a band marched to centerfield to play before a patriotic flag-raising ceremony, it was discovered that no one had ordered a flag.

Then the Dodgers went out and lost their first three games to the Phillies, all by the score of 1–0.

Those same Phillies started the season *very* well, much to McGraw's consternation. Philadelphia led the league through June, in fact, and McGraw never missed an opportunity to snipe at them.

"If a team like the Phillies can win a pennant in the National League, then the League is a joke," McGraw told the *Sporting News* in late July, a quote designed to be read in the City of Brotherly Love. And actually, by that time, New York had moved ahead of Philadelphia in the standings.

But not without a fight. Literally.

The Giants had slipped in front of the Phils on June 30 by beating Philadelphia at their ramshackle Huntington Avenue home, 11–10 in eleven innings. Accounts of the game could be found on the sports pages. Accounts of the rest of the day could be found in the Philadelphia police blotter.

During the game, McGraw, coaching third base for the Giants, had exchanged a barrage of particularly vile insults with Philadelphia pitcher Ad Brennan.

There is little doubt that McGraw provoked the incident. But after the game, as fans milled with players on the field, Brennan continued it by attacking McGraw and knocking him to the ground. No one was seriously hurt, and both McGraw and Brennan were eventually fined and suspended by the league. But McGraw had pumped up his team, which proceeded to sweep the entire four-game series from the Phils, an event that kept Philadelphia chasing New York for the rest of the season.

It was not the last incident in Philadelphia, however. A controversy surrounding a forfeit due to fan behavior on August 30 at the same Huntington Avenue grounds resulted in the Giants having to fight their way off the field to the clubhouse, then to the Broad Street railroad station. Giant Buck Herzog suffered a cut cheek and outfielder Red Murray had a pistol waved in his face before the police pushed the Giants into the train and sent them back to the more urbane and civilized atmosphere of New York City.

There, in the friendly Polo Grounds—paced by Mathewson, Marquard, and Jeff Tesreau who won seventy games among them—the Giants continued to vanquish all challengers, eventually leaving the Phillies in the second-place dust, twelve and a half games behind.

The Giants thus won their third straight pennant. Over these three championship years, there was little question which National League team had the dominant pitching. Mathewson and Marquard had phenomenally similar records, Matty being 74–36 for the three years, and Rube being 73–28. In this particular year of 1913, Matty also put on an exhibition of pitching control that has never been matched. The great Matty threw sixty-eight consecutive innings between June 19 and July 18 without issuing a single base on balls. Overall, Mathewson gave up only twenty-one walks all year in 306 innings, a feat of pitching placement not only unmatched but almost unimagined ever since.

But this baseball season of 1913 was also a time when Rube Marquard hit full stride in terms of self-confidence and perhaps even raw egotism—at least when the tonsillitis and Joe Kane's lawyers and process servers weren't harassing him. Here was his third great year in a row, the final installment in the trilogy of seasons that would eventually land him in baseball's Hall of Fame. At the time, the future seemed limitless.

Yet overall, 1913 proved to be a big year for several pitchers, even those who hadn't had as interesting a winter of 1912–13 as Rube. Seven National League hurlers won more than twenty games. The statistics of the day gave Marquard a 24–10 record (subsequently reduced to 23–10) which put him among a three-man team on the

Giants who had won twenty. Mathewson was 25–11 and Tesreau was 22–13. The second place Phillies had no such effective third starter, which probably cost them a more serious run at the pennant. But their top two men, Tom Seaton (27–12) and Grover Alexander (22–8) notched forty-nine wins between them.

In the American League, six pitchers won twenty games. But Mathewson's, Alexander's, and Marquard's records that year, as well as those of almost every other pitcher, were drawfed by the great Walter Johnson. Johnson had as stellar a year as was ever enjoyed by any pitcher.

Savor this: Thirty-six wins. Seven losses. Thirty complete games. Eleven shutouts. Three hundred forty-six innings pitched, 243 strikeouts. An ERA of 1.14 and, sprinkled in, the Big Train had three saves. The number-two man on the staff, Joe Boehling was 17–7. Beyond that for Washington was disaster. Aside from Johnson and Boehling, twenty-two other men pitched for the Nats that year, including forty-three-year-old Clark Griffith. The not-so-great twenty-two contributed to an impressively un-impressive 45–50 record. Still, Washington finished second behind the Philadelphia A's by only six and a half games. Like the Phillies, they could have easily used a third quality starter. And like the Phillies, cheapskate management was unwilling to shell out for just such a quality player.

It is this era of great pitching that Babe Ruth, one year away from joining the Boston Red Sox in 1914, would always remember.

"When I first broke in baseball was a defensive game," Ruth—or at least his ghostwriter—said in 1928. "Walter Johnson was in his prime then. And so was (Grover) Alexander, Marquard, and Eddie Plank. Those boys could pitch, believe me!"

Had the Phillies managed to beat the Giants for the National League pennant, they would have afforded Philadelphia the chance to be the second city to host the entire World Series. Chicago had hosted in 1906, St. Louis would host in 1944, and New York would host for the first of many times in 1921. Instead, Marquard, Mathew-son, McGraw, and the rest of the Giants found their old nemesis, the Philadelphia A's, waiting for them in October.

The A's of Connie Mack were playing in their third World Series in four years. They would prove once again to be an ornery opponent.

McGraw made the decision to "save" Mathewson past the first game, figuring that if the series went seven games, he'd be better off with Marquard, twenty-three, starting the final game, rather than Mathewson, thirty-three.

The strategy backfired.

Before thirty-six thousand grumbling fans at the Polo Grounds, Rube lost his stuff in the fourth inning of the first game, giving up three runs as well as a 1–0 Giant lead. Then in the fourth inning, the routine Giant killer Frank "Home Run" Baker unloaded another of his round trippers into the right field bleachers. The Giants rallied, but still lost 6–4. It could be argued that Rube, burned by Baker twice in three Octobers, contributed as much to the latter's Hall of Fame status as any pitcher.

Giving an indication of how the series might have gotten off on a better foot for the Giants, Mathewson came back the next day at Shibe Park in Philadelphia and pitched a gorgeous ten-inning shutout. The opposing pitcher was Eddie Plank, who had split two decisions against the Giants in 1911. The matchup of Mathewson against Plank was of further note as the two men had pitched against each other during their university days, Mathewson at Bucknell and Plank at Gettysburg College.

The next day, back in New York, the A's took control of the series again. A twenty-year-old rookie, Ambrose "Bullet Joe" Bush, a former Marquard teammate at Indianapolis in 1908, shut down the Giants while the A's roughed up Jeff Tesreau to go ahead in the Series, 2–1.

Al Demaree, later to become a critically acclaimed sports cartoonist for the *Sporting News*, started Game Four for the Giants and Philadelphia got to him for four runs in four innings. Attempting to stop the bloodletting, McGraw countered by sending Marquard in to relieve. The A's took Rube to task for two more runs, then hung on when the Giants started to come back. The A's won the game, 6–5 and led the series, 3–1.

The next day Mathewson pitched again in New York as the Giants hoped their ace could help them claw their way back into the series. But future Hall of Famer Eddie Plank had his own ideas, holding the Giants to one unearned run. Mathewson allowed two earned runs and three in total. The World Series was over, and John McGraw's Giants had lost three fall classics in a row.

There was also a bit of melodrama on the field after Game Five.

After Larry Doyle had popped up to end the series, Mathewson walked slowly across the playing grounds to the clubhouse at the far edge of centerfield. The friendly New York crowd converged on Matty. Those closest to him attempted to console him in defeat. Art Fromme, the Giants pitcher, who hadn't played at all in the series, joined Mathewson on the long walk. The crowd gently gave way before them.

Nearing the clubhouse, Fromme placed a mackinaw across Mathewson's sturdy shoulders. But as Matty climbed the steps to the clubhouse, the coat came loose, slid from him, and lay on the ground. Matty entered the clubhouse and closed the door behind him.

It was a strange vision, and one that haunted those who saw it. It gathered a certain eeriness through the years, carrying as it did a sense of finality, an image of royalty leaving behind its mantle, and, beneath the leaden New York skies, a sense of gloom.

What witnesses had seen, as it turned out, was Christy Mathewson's last appearance in a World Series — though no one could possibly have imagined it at the time. Big Six had started eleven World Series games and completed ten — still a record eighty-four years later — thrown shutouts in four of them — another record — and compiled an ERA of 1.15 with only ten walks in more than one hundred innings.

Yet he had but one World Championship — the one in 1905 — to show for it. And his won-loss record was 5–5.

On four different occasions unearned runs had cost him victories.

McGraw was unpredictable as ever in the bitterness of his third straight World Series loss. He congratulated Connie Mack lavishly. "You've got the greatest infield I've ever seen," McGraw told the A's skipper. "You deserved to win."

Then, after praising an old adversary, McGraw set about to lose an old friend.

Immediately after the end of the series, McGraw and coach Wilbert Robinson, who had been so instrumental in transforming Rube Marquard into a winning pitcher, attended a reunion of old Baltimore Orioles at a New York saloon.

McGraw could put away booze as well as anyone and on this sodden evening, he was intent on demonstrating it.

"Generally he (McGraw) knew his limit," wrote the noted baseball historian Charles Alexander in his outstanding biography, *John McGraw*. "The trouble was that on those occasions when he exceeded it, he became surly and belligerent." Surely, this was one of those nights.

After too many drinks, McGraw began to criticize Robinson's job on the coaching lines that afternoon. Robinson, somewhat affably and somewhat defensively, responded that McGraw had made more mistakes in managing in the series than everyone else in the series combined — a point of view quietly echoed by others, who questioned many of McGraw's strategies against the A's.

In a rage, McGraw fired his old friend and Oriole

teammate on the spot. Robinson retorted by throwing a glass of beer at McGraw, then left after the prerequisite brawl. Within another year, Robinson would be hired to manage the Brooklyn club, thus intensifying the tone for the interborough rivalry that would grow between the two clubs. Robinson and McGraw would not speak to each other again until shortly before Robinson's death in 1932.

"For eighteen years," baseball historian Lee Allen once wrote, referring to the eventual tenure of Robinson as manager of the Brooklyn club, "McGraw and Robinson would glare at each other from opposing dugouts."

But in the meantime, the baseball season of 1913 had finally concluded. And the fall season along Broadway was set to begin. Seeley, leaving her newborn at home with a nurse, was ready to take the stage again with her husband, with a new act, and new aspirations. The fifty-thousand-dollar alienation of affection suit filed by Kane against Marquard, however, remained unsettled.

13

◆

The Giants may have lost a third straight World Series, but Rube Marquard had lost none of his personal glitter. Even as a married man, Rube remained a heartthrob in Manhattan. Tall, slender, and dark complexioned, Marquard had grown more handsome and more self-assured by 1913. He was no longer a rookie and no longer a kid from the Midwest. He and his wife were self-assured Manhattanites.

"Rube dresses like a prince," opined the *Sporting News*, the well-known "Baseball Bible" (or, to its detractors, the "Baseball Babble"). "And Blossom is as lovely a woman as to be seen."

With Blossom on his arm, they formed one of the most attractive and most visible couples around the city. Together they were regulars at the top restaurants around Times Square — though Rube was something of an anomaly as he never smoked or consumed alcohol.

During the first years of their courtship and marriage, Marquard and Seeley were also never far from the daily glitter of stardom. If Rube wasn't pitching, then Blossom was performing. Or, in the off-season, such as the fall of 1913, they were performing together, selling out another of New York's big vaudeville houses.

Blossom, perhaps from having been a child entertainer, had a very firm sense of herself and her abilities, probably far more than many women of her day. She was thus attracted to the highly visible, highly vocal women's suffrage movement that was gaining political momentum by 1913. It was thus not surprising that the Marquard and Seeley sketch that would play the Palace Theater in 1913 — the most famous venue in vaudeville — would draw from the suffrage movement.

But first there was the unfinished business with Joe Kane.

In mid-October, Marquard was entered in a Ping-Pong tournament in one of the sports and exhibition halls around Times Square. Marquard was doing quite well, pocketing hundreds of dollars per game in prize money and bets. He had just added to his bankroll on the afternoon of October 15, when who should appear at the Ping-Pong parlor than Joe Kane and his insufferable mouthpiece, Nicholas Selvaggi. Kane and the lawyer wanted to discuss that long-standing matter of the $50,000 alienation of affection suit against Marquard.

Marquard, by this time, was in the habit of developing a sharp headache whenever Kane or Selvaggi appeared. Today was no exception. What was different was that Kane and Selvaggi began to press Marquard for some sort of settlement then and there. And as it happened,

Rube Marquard at the
height of his game as a
Giant in 1911.

Christy Mathewson,
young and handsome,
circa 1902.

Wilbert Robinson, as manager of the Brooklyn club in the 1920s
(above left). A trade ad for Rube's silent film, *Rube Marquard Wins,*
with the ever-lovely Alice Joyce *(above right)*.
(New York Public Library)

Three Giants, 1905. Manager John J. McGraw is flanked by
Mathewson, left, and Iron Man McGinnity, right.

JOE KANE

Now Playing Opposite to

Max Rogers

"**In Panama**"

A paid ad in *Variety* announced Joe Kane in *In Panama*, November 1908.

The winter of 1912–13 frequently found Blossom Seeley and Rube Marquard linked in the press by name, photograph and story.

Sheet music for "The Marquard Glide," as performed by Blossom and Rube.

Broadway cartoonists had a ball with McGraw, Seeley and Marquard in the autumn of 1912. This one's from the *New York Herald*.

A good vaudeville bill gave the customer a lot for as little as a dime. In March 1913, San Francisco's Orpheum Theater offered everything from an anteater to "Marquard & Seeley." During this engagement, Rube and Blossom were married.

Rube and Blossom, now married, but headliners again in 1913.

Blossom going the glamour route, as a star in the 1920s.

Rube could always find new fans, even at age 43, coaching and occasionally pitching for Atlanta in the Southern Association. Note the great hair styles. (Wide World Photos)

Rube also always knew where the money was. As a pari-mutuel clerk, he worked the $50 window. Rube is seen here at Garden State Park, Camden, New Jersey, September 1947. (Wide World Photos)

Still smiling after all these years. Benny Fields and Blossom
Seeley open at the Coconut Grove in Los Angeles,
November 1952. (Wide World Photos)

A constellation of southpaws: L–R, Rube, Stan Musial, Sandy
Koufax and Whitey Ford collect awards from the New York
Baseball Writer's Association, February 1964. Rube's
was a retroactive award as Player of the
Year for 1912. (Wide World Photos)

thanks to the suckers at the Ping-Pong fronton, Rube was flush with cash.

Not fifty grand. But enough.

"You want to settle?" Marquard finally barked before a crowd that quickly gathered. "You want cash? I'll settle for what I have on me."

Whether or not it was a real suggestion when Marquard made it would never be known. But as Rube started to empty the thick green contents of his pockets, it became an actual offer.

Kane, Selvaggi, and Marquard then repaired to a quiet Ping-Pong table and started to talk business. Within another few minutes, Rube had piled $2,254.78 on the table in cash and loose change. Every dime that was on him.

Kane—who once thought he was doing well when he was collecting sixty bucks a week as an agent—felt his eyes go wide. This was, after all, the era when an auto worker was looking for a five-dollar-a-day salary for nine sweaty hours on the assembly line.

Marquard's eyes found Kane's. "Take it," the pitcher said, "or leave it."

Joe barely had to think. "I'll take it," he said.

In return, Marquard received a paper from Kane acknowledging the payment essentially in exchange for Blossom's services as a wife. Marquard filed the paper in court the next day, causing Kane's $50,000 lawsuit to be discontinued. In the bargain, Rube would never have to explain to a State Supreme Court justice exactly why— and how—he had lured another man's wife into his own

bed. For approximately four cents on the dollar,
Marquard had claimed himself a wife. In terms of Joe
Kane, Rube and Blossom were now free and clear.

Marquard and Seeley opened their 1913 vaudeville tour
at the Palace Theater in the first week of November. And
once again, they were a smash. Their skit this fall was
titled *The Suffragette Pitcher*, and the work was another
creation of Thomas Gray and Ray Walker, who had concocted the last season's piece of mischief for Rube and
Blossom. The show picked up where the previous year's
show had left off, working in a baseball motif with timely
jokes, some self-effacing humor, and a handful of new
songs. The show ran nine minutes and was placed in the
starring spot on the Palace's bill. (Sharing the spotlight
were a man named Joseph Jefferson, whose specialty was
impersonating Rip Van Winkle, and a nimble musician
named Volant who played a piano that was swinging
from wires and which swung wildly across the stage.)

The show was once again a sellout and audiences
were wildly enthusiastic. *Variety* carried a long review
that caught the full spirit of Marquard and Seeley's new
piece as well as the time:

> Rube Marquard may be traded to Boston
> or some other team before next season, but
> that won't keep him from adding to the
> family's coffers with his present vaude-
> villing with his wife, Blossom Seeley.
> Rube's regular craft is pitching, and he's

a good one when he is right. Rube was off color in the recent World Series, but still hangs onto that "world's record nineteen straight."

That Rube had tough luck against the Athletics is made the butt of some hearty puns in the skit that Rube and Miss Seeley have at the Palace this week. Blossom has not done any stage work since long back. In the "Suffragette" offering, she does the bulk of the talking and singing.

She sang a new song, "My Baseball Man," written by Tommy Gray and Raymond Walker, which fits her like a glove. (It is the number she should make the most of.) The skit has Blossom as the owneress of a female nine who rings Rube in the big game in female garb. For several minutes pictures are shown of Rube and Blossom playing the game at the Polo Grounds, before empty seats. Rube is finally discovered and is chased off the field. They clamber onto the stage for a little chatter and a song. Oh, yes, they did a little dance which Blossom said took her all summer to teach him. The biggest laugh came when Miss Seeley remarked, "I'd put you in to pitch, Rube, if you had a good game left in you."

Another resulted when Rube kidded

himself about the baseball articles he wrote. The dialogue opens in Mr. and Mrs. Rube's apartment, where Rube is doing the hash slinging stunt. Tommy Gray has given the pair the best act they have yet had. It should pass on the road as well as in New York houses. Rube's still a curiosity by reason of his Giants connection, while Blossom has the ability to entertain without any call on the Marquard diamond prestige to aid her.

Marquard and Seeley had the best spot on the Palace program.

Other reviews concurred. But an interesting subtext also began to appear in some of the write-ups.

"As a dancer," grumbled one critic, "Rube Marquard remains one of the great left-handed pitchers."

"Marquard and Seeley are utterly gracious and charming," said another, "but on stage it is Miss Seeley who carries the day."

And then there were a few scribblers who liked to damn with faint praise.

"Mr. Marquard seems to get as much fun out of his singing and dancing as does the audience," wrote a second reviewer in *Variety*. "But while Rube is onstage, you can't help but remark that his given name is well chosen."

In other words, the critics were starting to take the gloves off with Rube Marquard. A novelty act is one thing, they seemed to be saying, but if the lanky southpaw from Cleveland was going to come out each autumn, go onstage and rake in a lot of money, he was going to be judged by the standards of any other professional actor.

Rube didn't miss the direction in which these comments were going. And it gave him pause to consider what he was doing. Their new act played several theaters in New York through December, including a special "Baseball Week" at Proctor's Fifth Avenue Theater where the vaudeville bill was heavily laden with acts with baseball associations: Charley Dooin, the captain of the Phillies, appeared and sang "songs of 'ould' Ireland," for example, and Cap Anson—billed as "the father of the game"—stumbled his way through a poem. Naturally, however, *The Suffragette Pitcher* took top billing.

Rube and Blossom ended their New York appearances just before Christmas and took time to be home together on Riverside Drive with their infant son. Blossom's mother lived in New York at the time and frequently contributed to the child's care. The couple spent a happy Christmas—Rube ran up a tidy bill for jewelry for his wife—and celebrated a quiet New Year to welcome 1914.

The whole Kane-Marquard-Seeley episode, however, though legally at rest, was not without one last gasp, and one bizarre final twist.

Rube and Blossom visited Atlantic City shortly after the New Year of 1914 had come in. Kane, still playing the part of the jilted cuckolded spouse, had determined a final method of harassing them.

On January fourth, Kane, learning that Marquard and

Seeley were in Atlantic City, contacted the magistrate who had issued the warrant for their arrest a year earlier. The warrant was still active. Kane asked that it be served. Served it was. And the newspaper headlines looked *very* familiar. They almost read like theater reviews, but then again the distinction had always been vague when it came to Marquard and Seeley:

RUBE MARQUARD IS UNDER ARREST
New York Telegraph

GIANTS' MARQUARD ARRESTED
New York Times

MARQUARD AND SEELEY ARRESTED
Variety

Marquard and Seeley, were thus arrested by Atlantic City police on the charges of having an adulterous liaison at the Hotel Dunlop two Octobers earlier. Rube and Blossom—promptly, angrily, and indignantly—posted $500 bail, pending a hearing later in the month.

Rube and Blossom were now married and Kane never came forward to press any further charges. Similarly, there were no witnesses to the Dunlop incident who wished to testify. So the case was quickly dismissed at a hearing three weeks later. But not, of course, without Kane having managed to harass Rube and Blossom a final time. Obviously, Kane thought it would be a fine bit of mischief to place their names in the newspapers again and gain a small final measure of retribution, though the free scandal-tinged publicity did nothing to hurt their touring show, which was now headed toward Boston and Chicago.

"The action of Kane causing the old warrant to be served causes a good deal of surprise," wrote an observer in an unsigned article in the *Dramatic News*.

Indeed, it did. And somehow the correspondent, in discussing the uselessness of serving the warrant, managed to write his entire article without using the phrase "sour grapes" even once.

14

---◆---

Late in 1912, when McGraw had been performing in vaudeville in Chicago, the Giants manager had struck up a friendship with Charles Comiskey, previously a rival player during McGraw's tempestuous journey through the American League, and now owner of the White Sox.

Kicking back one night in a Windy City watering hole, McGraw and Comiskey starting talking about Albert Spalding's around-the-world baseball tour of 1888–89, a public relations coup for Spalding and an effort—moderately successful—to bring baseball to what was then deemed less enlightened sections of the planet. The fact that Spalding sold baseballs and other equipment to the new converts played no small part in his missionary zeal.

McGraw and Comiskey, after much booze and hypothesizing, decided they should make a similar journey, rounding up Giants players and White Sox players, plus whomever else they needed, to make the trip. Over the next several months, mostly during the baseball season of 1913, plans took shape. Marquard was invited, but being a new father and a new husband and having lucrative vaudeville commitments to bring *The Suffragette Pitcher* before an appreciative public, he declined.

For the ballplayers who would make the journey, however, the trip began in October 1913, shortly after the close of the World Series. The plans were for the Giants and White Sox to barnstorm across the U.S., playing exhibitions, and earning enough money to finance the rest of the trip. It didn't quite work out that way, with receipts eventually being less than expected. But the trip did proceed.

McGraw and Comiskey's band crossed the American continent by the end of November, having played thirty-one games. Included was one in Sioux City, Iowa, where hundreds of Native Americans from a nearby reservation turned out to cheer Chief Meyers and Jim Thorpe of the Giants. Then the party of sixty-seven—which included a film crew for an outfit quixotically named Eclectic Pictures—took a small Canadian Pacific steamer up to Vancouver where one final baseball game was played on the North American continent.

Embarking on a road trip to end all road trips, the steamer next turned east and began a long, cold, arduous seven-thousand-mile trek to Japan, where they arrived twenty-three gray days after leaving Canada.

But they were welcomed enthusiastically. University teams had introduced baseball to Japan several years earlier and the Japanese had already caught "baseball fever" of the 1913 variety.

From Japan, the voyagers continued to Shanghai, Hong Kong, Manila, and Australia. They crossed the In-

dian Ocean, stopped in Ceylon, then continued up
through the Suez Canal to Cairo, then made a side ex-
cursion to Giza to play a desert baseball game in the
shadow of the Sphinx, just as Spalding had in 1889. From
there they continued to Europe—Italy, France, and England.

In Italy, the Catholic players obtained an audience
with Pope Pius X. In France, McGraw and several others
dropped a bundle at the casinos, and in England they
played a baseball game before King George V. They then
traveled home from Liverpool on the British liner
Lusitania, the ill-fated luxury liner that would be sunk
by the Kaiser's submarines off the western coast of Ireland thirteen months later.

The trip had taken 139 days. And much had happened
as the Giants had traveled.

A group of aggressive sportsmen-businessmen,
equipped with high hopes and bags of money, were trying to transform a midwestern minor league, known as
the Federal League, into a third major circuit. And they
now were causing a lot of ripples. Already they were set
to go head to head against the National and American
Leagues in Chicago, St. Louis, Pittsburgh, and Brooklyn
in 1914, and had added such attractive other venues as
Baltimore, Kansas City, and Indianapolis. Now, in the
spring of 1914, all the Feds needed were major league
players. So the talent raids began in earnest. And there
was nothing subtle about them. When the Giants and
White Sox players returned to New York harbor on that
snowy March 6, emissaries from the Federal League used

tug boats to meet the *Lusitania* before she even docked, and began showing suitcases filled with money to the players.

Any big-name player was a prime target. So was McGraw, who was offered an astounding one hundred thousand dollars *guaranteed* to manage a Newark franchise in the Federal League.

Mathewson was offered a huge sum, too, but — symbol of rectitude that he was — he turned the money down, though not without considerable thought. The deal Mathewson was offered would have had him pitching and managing the Brooklyn club. Ty Cobb, Tris Speaker, and Walter Johnson turned the Feds down, too, but not without significant raises from their respective plantation owners in Detroit, Boston, and Washington. The Feds did, however, sign Joe Tinker and "Three Finger" Brown of the Cubs, and Eddie Plank and Chief Bender of the Philadelphia A's.

Marquard, coming off his three huge seasons, and bringing with him tons of publicity, was actively courted also. Being a freer spirit than many players, Rube listened intently. But he also had fallen into a salary "trap" that the Giants had set for their players.

McGraw and owner Harry Hempstead had anticipated the eventual raids of the Feds and had locked in their key players with generous — for the time, at least — contracts. The salaries had even been sweetened for the last few years by World Series checks and post-season exhibition games against the Yankees. Hence, even though the Feds actually played a schedule in 1914, the

Giants would lose only two marginal players, Otis Crandall and Art Wilson, both of whom were quickly replaced by trades. However, the waltzing courtship between the Federal League and Rube Marquard would continue at a later date.

The 1914 season would prove a memorable one for the Giants, but not necessarily favorably. No sooner had McGraw ensconced himself in Marlin, Texas, for spring training, than he indulged in one of his legendary brawls, this one with a Texas League manager (and former St. Louis Browns first baseman) named Pat Newman. Newman, a husky six footer, clearly got the best of McGraw, judging by the bandages on McGraw's split lower lip.

This was also the year that, in spring training, McGraw got his first view of a nineteen-year-old left-handed pitcher who'd been signed by Jack Dunn's Baltimore Orioles of the International League. The kid pitcher, George Herman Ruth, was fresh out of St. Mary's Industrial School, and greatly impressed McGraw in a spring training game against the Giants.

McGraw asked Dunn, an old Oriole, to give McGraw the first chance to buy the young pitcher. Dunn agreed, or at least McGraw always insisted Dunn had. Later in the baseball season, however, in mid-July, Dunn offered Ruth to Connie Mack. Mack exercised the type of baseball judgment that would lead the Philadelphia A's to seven straight cellar finishes from 1915 through 1921, and referred Dunn to Joseph Lannin, owner of the Red Sox.

Boston would buy the young star, only to deal him to the Yankees by the end of the decade, where he would more than haunt, taunt, and infuriate McGraw. "McGraw," wrote baseball historian Charles Alexander, "would never forgive Dunn for what he considered a broken promise."

It could also be argued that the sale of Ruth to the Yankees put in motion a long chain of events that moved the Giants, once New York's most popular and most glamorous sports franchise, all the way to San Francisco's Candlestick Park. When Ruth became a Yankee he turned the Yankees into a bigger draw in New York than the Giants. McGraw eventually evicted the Yankees, his tenants, from the Polo Grounds, whereupon they built Yankee Stadium and became for many years the richest and most successful franchise in American sports. The Giants became New York's "second team" and eventually chose to move west.

When the 1914 baseball season began, however, the New York Giants once again looked to have the best talent in the National League. Mathewson, though thirty-four years old, appeared to be throwing well in spring training. So did Marquard, now twenty-four, and considered by most of the sporting world to be Mathewson's heir apparent on baseball's most successful club.

Anyone looking very closely, however, might have seen some clouds on the horizon, portents of little storms that would eventually endanger the Giants' quest for an unprecedented forth straight National League pennant. Far from the headlines of the day, for example, Rube and Blossom were already starting to have some serious

discussions at home about whose career was more important and exactly how to make their marriage work.
Keeping alive a white-hot romance was one thing. Building a successful marriage on a day-to-day basis was another.

Marquard had reported to Texas without his wife and
was soon less than pleased about the turn of events. Their
tour together during the 1913–14 season had been enormously successful in terms of audience and money, even
though there had been rumblings of critical discontent
about Rube. But upon Rube's departure for Texas, Blossom immediately switched gears from the "mixed" act of
Marquard & Seeley to just plain Blossom Seeley. She barely
missed a breath. Or a beat. Back she went to the Victoria,
singing songs for which she had secured the sole performing rights — a sly business move: if an audience wanted to
hear a certain new "hit" song, they had to pay to hear
Blossom sing it. Shortly afterward she went on tour. And
even though motherhood was firmly upon her, she continued to hit the sex symbol buttons by appearing in
gowns that set male heads to spinning in the audience.

"Miss Seeley sang of 'Diaphanous Diana,'" noted a
Chicago critic in a review in May 1914, "whose pedes-
trian trips along the street caused a general masculine
shading of the eyes."

Yet the critic hadn't shaded his own eyes, which must
have been popping. "Miss Seeley's gown is rather Diana-
like," he raved, "to say the least."

Seeley's tour continued into the summer, which occasionally put no small stress on her marriage. There were

times when Marquard was in New York and his wife was not, and no man in the year of 1914 would have been pleased with such a development. Certainly Rube wasn't. And as the 1914 season lumbered along toward disaster, the home arrangements began taking their toll on Rube.

The Giants moved into first place in May as their two main rivals, Pittsburgh and Cincinnati, started to fold. Brooklyn, now managed by Wilbert Robinson, looked to be an improved club, but not one that would figure in this pennant race. Mathewson continued to win. Matty would finish the year at 24–13 with five shutouts. But there were those who insisted—correctly, as it turned out—that the old zip wasn't there. Jeff Tesreau would have a career year, winning twenty-six games and carrying the club for much of the season. But Marquard was struggling. And the problems at home had to have had their effect.

Going into late May, Rube was barely better than a .500 pitcher. Recalling how he had struggled earlier in his career, however, most observers expected him to turn things around with a long streak. He was, after all, just two seasons removed from his famous Nineteen Straight and was one of the most famous pitchers in baseball. So, other than the domestic problems, there was no *real* visible reason to worry. Then again, in an age when medical science had addressed very little about the mysteries of a pitcher's arm, it *was* possible to just lose one's skills sometimes. Smoky Joe Wood had dropped from thirty-four wins in 1912 to nine in 1913, for example. So Rube most likely had more sleepless nights than he had admitted.

June arrived.

Marquard and Seeley saw each other when possible. Then on June 28, world events shoved baseball to the back of most people's thoughts, even in the safety of Fortress America. On that day in Sarajevo, a Bosnian nationalist murdered Archduke Franz Ferdinand of Austria and his wife, setting in motion the events that would lead mankind into what was then the worst war in the history of civilization. Within another six weeks, all of the conflicting parties of Europe would be at war and President Woodrow Wilson would be making grave but ominous statements about American neutrality. It was a jittery time in America: a significant part of the population was of German extraction and openly sympathetic to the Kaiser, while much of the rest of American society was pro-British.

In mid-July, however, just weeks before the guns of August changed the face of the world, Marquard was nursing a 10–10 record and not doing an awful lot to help the Giants remain in front of the Chicago Cubs. Few people were paying any attention to the Boston Braves, a traditional National League doormat, who had been mired — deservedly — in the league's basement as usual on July 4. The funny thing was that the Braves suddenly started to win under their fiery manager George Stallings. Stallings was a man whose vocabulary was so vile that it would have made a chief petty officer blush.

Throughout his career, Marquard usually had an easy time with Pittsburgh. And throughout his great seasons of 1911, 1912, and 1913, he was frequently in the habit of making a specific announcement on the days he was pitching.

"Boys," he'd say to his teammates, "this is Pittsburgh. Just get me one run. That's all I need to win."

In one game against the Pirates on July 17, the Giants trailed 1–0 going to the ninth. Then they scored the run that Rube had requested. Marquard and the opposing pitcher, Babe Adams, then traded goose eggs through another nine innings. Marquard, on the bench between innings, grew increasingly cranky, asking over and over for "one more run."

Finally the Giants scored twice in the twenty-first inning. Marquard gained the complete game victory, but continued his growling in the locker room afterward, even though he was now in the record books for a complete game victory in what was then the longest game in baseball history.

Larry Doyle, the longtime shortstop, stopped by Marquard's locker. "What you never told us," Doyle said, "was what inning you wanted the runs."

McGraw was said to have greatly admired Rube's poise and stamina in staying with such a long dramatic effort. And surely McGraw was paying more attention to his own pitching staff than to the upstart Braves, who had now climbed all the way up to fifth place. But in truth and in retrospect, Marquard's twenty-one-inning effort might be seen as a turning point in Marquard's career—and not a good one. With a record of 11–10, Rube then went on a long streak as everyone had hoped. But it was the wrong kind.

For almost the entire rest of the season, Rube
Marquard could not win a game. On the mound he was
erratic and inconsistent. When Rube pitched well, the
Giants didn't score. Five times he was on the losing end
of shutouts. When the Giants did score, Rube looked as
if he were chucking batting practice.

This continued through August and into September
until the erratic and unpredictable Rube eventually had a
streak of twelve consecutive losses, an accomplishment
that definitely would *not* be worked into any upcoming
vaudeville routine. It was only on September 26, on Marquard's last start of the year, that he managed to stagger
to a 13–6 win over his old cousins, the Pirates. The win
brought his season's record to a thoroughly untidy and
unimpressive 12–22. The word "lemon" again started to
make its appearance in the ever-fickle New York sports
pages.

Worse, the word "miracle" was also starting to appear.

Those lowly Braves, who would win forty-eight of
their last sixty-four games and thirty-four of their final
forty-four, had soared from the league's outhouse to the
league's penthouse, passing the Giants on September 2
and nudging the New York team into second place. Suddenly, the ever-vile George Stallings was a "Miracle Man"
and these were the "Miracle Braves."

On September 7, and now tied with the Braves for
first place, the Giants went to Boston and played two
games against the Braves, a Labor Day doubleheader. The
twin bill was played with separate admissions tickets in

the morning and the afternoon. The Braves rented Fenway Park for the occasion, rather than use their usual field, rickety little South End Grounds with its limited seating. A total of seventy thousand fans paid their way into the two games, an astonishing fact considering that even then the Red Sox were the golden children of Boston sports and the Braves were almost always last in attendance in both leagues.

But no matter. This was a Miracle Year. Mathewson lost the morning game, 5–4. But big Jeff Tesreau came back and led the Giants to a 10–1 win in the afternoon contest. The second game featured a brawl between Giants outfielder Fred Snodgrass and Braves pitcher Lefty Tyler.

The brawl had a memorable scenario. Tyler plunked Snodgrass with a fastball. Snodgrass, from a perch at first base, responded with a single finger raised in a universal gesture of ill will. Tyler responded—to the delight of the Boston fans—with a pantomime rendition of Snodgrass's muffed catch that "cost" the Giants the 1912 World Series. The two men met midway between first base and the pitcher's mound to discuss things further. Somehow, a fistfight quickly followed.

When Snodgrass went to centerfield in the bottom of the inning, a shower of pop bottles greeted him. Several Giants went to centerfield to aid their teammate. Then Boston's mayor, James Curley, ably working the crowd, went onto the field to demand that Snodgrass be removed from the game. Umpire Bill Klem refused, further inciting the fans.

The game was eventually completed. Boston and New York remained in a tie for the league lead at the end of the day. But the events of September 7 seemed to charge the Braves and enervate the Giants. New York could never get past the Braves again in the standings as Boston eventually roared to a pennant by ten and a half games over the second place New York squad.

Not yet finished with miracles, Boston then defeated the mighty Philadelphia A's—whom McGraw hadn't been able to beat in two of the last three world series—in four straight games. Connie Mack was so miffed—and so unwilling to compete with the Federal League in the payroll department—that he would sell off his stars at the end of the season, tightening his future grip on the American League basement.

All in all, this had been a disastrous season for the Giants in general and for Rube in particular. And very quickly, Rube started to see the flip side of being famous. Blossom was in demand onstage this fall and Rube, for the first time since the bleak winter of 1910, was not. Not only was the novelty off his act, but the luster was off his arm. It had to occur to him that a guy who had won seventy-three games over three seasons for a pennant winner looked a lot better prancing around in a tux and top hat than a guy who had just lost almost twice as often as he'd won for an also-ran team. The latter sort of guy might look a little, well, silly.

And then there was the matter of star billing.

Blossom was the real star onstage, and always would

be. Rube was along for the ride, even though the ride had been a spectacular one, and one that few men might ever take. But this was never so apparent as in the winter of 1914.

Rube stayed home. He told friends that he had received some small offers to perform but had turned them down. To other friends, he acknowledged that the strains — and distractions — of performing had finally caught up with him and had perhaps — *perhaps* — contributed to the disappointing season that had just ended. As evidence, he cited the fact that he had lost weight the previous winters and had ignored his training at the gym. He seemed to be saying that he had gotten away with these sins in the past but couldn't anymore.

But the stardom situation loomed just as large in his mind. He must have been thinking about it every time he stood in the wings of the theater watching Blossom play to a packed house and knock the audience dead. Blossom was the star and Rube was (again) a losing pitcher. He could see the attraction in the eyes of other men when they looked at her and — for the first time, maybe — he might have felt a little like Joe Kane had when the twenty-one-year-old Richard Marquard had happened on the scene.

Rube and Blossom traveled in the West over the off-season. They visited friends and family and discussed their future. The dialogues evolved to the point where a recurring subject soon became who should give up whose career for the other. Rube felt he needed a wife and his wife should be home, subservient to his own interests—an attitude certainly shared by a huge majority of men of the day, if not still.

Blossom replied that her skills, talents, and earning potential were unique, particularly for a woman. She made a compelling case, but not one that her husband wanted to hear.

So through the winter, the problem went unresolved. And if Rube could take any consolation, it was that his 12–22 record had barely diminished the interest the Federal League had in him. The Feds were still willing to throw big-time money at him and let him be the star of the Brooklyn club.

So again, he started to listen. Many of the players who had jumped to the Feds had made out like the proverbial bandits, at least financially. Even though some of the franchises were shaky, the owners still had deep pockets. The Brooklyn club was owned by Robert B. Ward, a millionaire baker best known for Tip Top Bread, a spongy white recipe that helped give white bread a bad reputation. Not surprisingly, the Brooklyn Feds were known colloquially as the Tip Tops.

Ward had, it could be said, more dough than he knew what to do with. And by Christmastime, Rube was listening to his offers with deepening seriousness.

Then the news hit the papers, as well as the Giants' front office. Rube, with a year remaining on his $8,500 per season contract with the New York Giants, had accepted a $1,500 bonus from the Brooklyn Tip Tops as part of a $10,000 salary the Feds would pay him for jumping leagues.

The signing, if it held up in court, was a major coup for the Federal League, which needed star power for their upcoming second season. Marquard gave the league exactly that, much the way the signing of Joe Namath would give glitter and credibility to the infant American Football League in the 1960s.

McGraw, however, still had plans for Marquard, despite the latter's erratic pitching, occasionally flaky behavior, and 12–22 record of the previous season. And the plans did not include seeing Rube pitch in the rival outlaw league. McGraw had to be thinking, when he wasn't busy raging, that he hadn't turned down a pile of money to jump leagues only to watch his best players *already under contract* desert his club.

There was no way, in other words, that Rube was leaving without a battle.

This is not to say that the end of the 1914 season was not without its diversions for Giant fans. Early September saw the release of a three-reel silent movie titled *Detective Swift*, and starring none other than John J. McGraw in the title role.

"The calm, enigmatic countenance of a baseball manager is a proper one for portraying a detective," commented the *Moving Picture World* at the outset of their favorable review — though the term "calm" applied to the tempestuous McGraw may have raised some eyebrows. Nonetheless, the critic hailed the film as one "that will please baseball fans everywhere and for that matter, picturegoers in general."

McGraw, who frequently ranted both publicly and privately about his players dabbling in the world of entertainment, might have won some sort of Do-As-I-Say-Not-As-I-Do award for his involvement in this flick. Nonetheless, even eight decades later, it has its amusing side.

The author of the scenario—one dares not use the word "script" for a silent movie—was a man named Frank McGlynn. McGlynn also played the villain, a piece of early-day Eurotrash named Jacques Renault, who also had an on-screen alias as one Count Otronski.

McGlynn-Renault-Otronski meets a society matron named Mrs. Henderson at the start of the film. Otronski poses as a continental *gentilhomme* for an evening, then does a cat burglar job on milady's residence the next morning at three a.m., swiping a pearl necklace that he had admired a few hours earlier.

Enter Detective Swift, who draws a bead on the ersatz count quicker than a Marquard fastball. The detective, who seemed to have a lot more on the ball than his real-life counterparts Kinzie and Carter in Atlantic City, is equipped with nothing more than his wits and a magnifying glass, à la Conan Doyle. But such tools are not to be dismissed.

Swift, a.k.a McGraw, takes up the case in a cool, confident manner and soon has traced the villain to a boardinghouse, exactly the type of lodgings where a fake count might live. But Otronski has flown the coop and now a chase around the world begins.

The Giants world tour in the fall of 1913 may have inspired what followed. Eclectic's cameras were rolling and the story quickly became secondary to the scenic effects, which for the day, were apparently quite spectacular—through Cairo, the Pyramids, and the Libyan desert. Along the way, someone even prevailed upon some real live Bedouins to engage in a conspiracy scene with Otronski, followed by a scene in which they detained McGraw.

But Detective Swift is not to be deterred, catching up with the nefarious count as the latter attempted to board a steamer for America. The necklace was recovered and Detective Swift reaped a significant financial reward, which he munificently turned over to a young maid in the Henderson household, a generous and democratic touch carefully designed to please the audiences of the day.

If only the baseball season had worked out as neatly.

There was also a macabre footnote to the year 1914. Rube Marquard's old friend and occasional bad influence Mike Donlin had deigned to stop by professional baseball again in 1912, this time with Pittsburgh. Donlin would leave again in 1913 to go back into vaudeville. But McGraw was desperate for some hitting in 1914, and Donlin, now desperate for a job, took a final three dozen at bats for the Giants in 1914, mostly as a pinch hitter.

Fortune by this time had treated Donlin both kindly and cruelly. Little Mabel Hite—his wife and vaudeville partner—had died of illness, both suddenly and tragically at age thirty. Not long afterward, Donlin, a man who couldn't be without female companionship very long, married another pretty young actress named Rita Ross.

Mike had also turned to the movies and begun a career as a supporting actor that would last for the rest of his life, until his death in 1933 in Hollywood.

Most of Mike Donlin's work was in silent films. He had a good career, but never impressed the critics. *Moving Picture World*, an early trade magazine in the film business, referred to him as "something of an actor." And the *New York Times*, in his obituary, sneaked in the opinion that as an actor Donlin was never quite as good as he thought he was. No matter: Mike wasn't around to see his final write-up.

One bizarre incident did follow him for many years, however. When Mabel Hite died, or was "booked out of town," as the Broadway slang of the time went, she was cremated. Her ashes were placed in an urn at a name-brand undertaking establishment in Manhattan. For some reason, the urn stayed there in a package for several years.

Then—by mistake or as a malicious prank—someone sent the package to Murray's Restaurant on West Forty-second Street. When the package arrived, there was a bomb scare, so the police soaked the package with water. When the package was opened, Mabel's waterlogged urn was found.

Mike sued for a ton of money and collected.

15

◆

In January 1915, as previously noted, Rube found himself in the midst of scandal and controversy. Several players had managed by this time to successfully jump to the Federal League, but none had Rube's star power. Perhaps more significantly, no other jumpers seemed to have signed two different contracts, one for the Federal League and one for the National League.

"The Brooklyn Feds made me a swell offer," Rube told sportswriter Tom Andrews of the *New York Times* in early January. "After being convinced that I was not tied to the New York Giants for life, I decided to better myself and accept."

What Rube was doing, in addition to breaking his contract with the Giants, was running smack up against baseball's reserve clause, which did indeed reserve the services of a player to a specific team for the duration of his career. The reserve system—a benefit to the owners and absolutely no one else—had been the cause of the great players' revolt of 1890 and would become the subject of court cases and controversy throughout the century. In 1915, Rube would have his own tilt with it.

"A ballplayer is worth what he can get and no more, and he can only play for a certain number of years," Marquard said, sounding a theme that would echo for decades. "There is no reason why he should not get the most obtainable, same as an actor. You know, the magnates themselves started the players jumping and have no one to blame but themselves."

Marquard then topped all of his thoughts on the reserve clause by stating that he had no intention of returning to the Giants . . . unless the courts told him that he had to.

When February arrived, Rube received a notice from the Giants demanding that he report to Marlin, Texas, in March for spring training as usual. The Giants reminded him that he was under contract, the one upon which Sinister Dick Kinsella had traveled across the U.S. to get Rube's left-handed signature. On the same day, Rube also received instructions from the Brooklyn Tip Tops to proceed to *their* spring training site in Wells, Mississippi. It was going to be damned hard to pitch for two teams at once, much less be in two spring training camps simultaneously. Something somewhere had to give.

"The errant pitcher," commented the stately *New York Times*, as it covered what New York fans now called the Marquard case, "has made a sad mess of things."

The wrangling among the Giants, the Tip Tops, and Rube continued into early March. Rube had once again displayed his remarkable talent at being a warring party in a triangle.

There were those who considered the whole episode a

clever publicity stunt. Could the Tip Tops, for example, have been the only sports observers in North America who had not known that Marquard was under contract to the Giants? Or had they merely wanted to see how far they could press the issue? Were they hoping that McGraw would finally pop his cork over Marquard and unload him?

If the latter sentiment had been a factor in their strategy, they might have been on the right track, considering how the remainder of the season turned out. But they were premature.

McGraw considered the Marquard situation a point of honor and the Giants readied their attorneys for litigation, a case they would surely have won, inasmuch as Rube had signed a binding contract with New York a year before the contract with Brooklyn. And the Tip Tops, had Rube misrepresented himself, could have sued the pants off their would-be hurler for the same reason. But the case never went as far as a courtroom.

McGraw eventually cut through the whole mess by telephoning Robert Ward and working out a deal. The Giants would reimburse Brooklyn for the $1,500 they had paid to Marquard in December if the Tip Tops would quit their claim to Rube.

Much to Rube's horror, Ward agreed. McGraw's problem southpaw then had little choice but to limp back to Marlin, Texas, and return to the Giants — the very vision of contrition. To make matters worse, Blossom stayed north and began a new solo act onstage. And the $1,500 eventually came out of Marquard's paycheck from the Giants.

Rube's case, however, did figure into the antitrust suit that the Federal League eventually brought against the National and American Leagues, a suit that attacked the very basis of professional baseball contracts, that dreaded reserve clause. An indication of how dear the clause has always been to the owners might have been their gratitude to Judge Kennesaw Mountain Landis, who gave major league baseball an antitrust exemption in 1918 after the Federal League folded. The owners then decided that Landis was their type of guy and rewarded the judge by making him baseball's first commissioner.

The season that followed would be a turning point for Rube Marquard both personally and professionally.

He was in one sense lucky, in that he still had his job with the Giants. The American and National Leagues had taken a beating in attendance the previous year, thanks primarily to competition from the Feds, who actually drew enough fans to hurt the two established leagues. So the sixteen owners of the American and National League clubs, always anxious to hit the players in a way that hurt, had passed a resolution trimming their rosters. Until minor leaguers could be called up in September, managers would have to get by with twenty-one players, four fewer than the previous total of twenty-five. If players hated this—sixteen percent of the major league jobs had unceremoniously been eliminated, after all— managers hated it even more. But in the days before a players' union, there was little the ballplayers could do other than grimace. It wasn't even wise to mouth off in public. Most of the sportswriters were beholden to the owners and the free lunches served in the press rooms at the ballparks. A player deemed a troublemaker could be ostracized from the game by the owner who controlled his contract simply by not signing him. No matter how much players might have compared their fate to working on a high-class chain gang — and some made exactly that analogy — it was better than a coal mine or a factory, the options open to most players.

Aside from that, a season that would quickly turn to ashes would open optimistically for the Giants.

Jess Tesreau, continuing his fine pitching from the previous season, easily beat the Brooklyn Robins — now so-named for their portly malaprop-prone manager, Uncle Robbie — on opening day at the Polo Grounds. A robust crowd of twenty-five thousand turned out on a fine mid-April day.

Then Marquard pitched the next day and delivered a receipt to the borough of Brooklyn, firing an impressive 2–0 *no-hitter* against the club of his former pitching coach. The no-hitter went a long way toward restoring some of Marquard's luster among Giant fans, who were generally angry with his threats to jump to the rival borough in the rival league. But no one at the time — least of all Rube — could have realized that the no-hitter — much like the long twenty-one inning victory against Babe Adams and the Pirates — would help seal his doom with the Giants.

"I didn't seem to be able to get going after I'd pitched that no-hitter in April," Marquard recalled years later.

This was another way of saying that he couldn't get

anyone out. In actuality, he was again erratic, brilliant some days, a busher on others. He split his next sixteen decisions with the Giants, but was not the same pitcher he had been two, three, and four seasons earlier when he won over 70 percent of his decisions. His ERA ballooned to the 3.60 range and McGraw exiled him to the bullpen.

These were enormously difficult times in the New York clubhouse. Favored to win the pennant, the entire team collapsed. Even the great Mathewson would fade away to an 8–14 record this year, signaling his decline from greatness. Longtime regulars like Snodgrass and Meyers appeared to have aged ten years apiece in one off-season.

The New York Giants took an unusual position in the league standings in May — the cellar — and astonishingly were still there when the season ended.

Meanwhile the Phillies — *the Phillies!* — gave their somnambulant city their first National League pennant. There was irony aplenty to go around. Not only had the "wrong" Philadelphia team found its way into the World Series, but Connie Mack's Athletics landed in the cellar at the same time as the Giants.

Sic transit gloria mundi.

McGraw and Connie Mack, rivals in the World Series so recently, looked far less brilliant as managers of eighth-place clubs in eight-team leagues. No one, in 1915, suggested that the A's and Giants play at the end of the season.

But just because the Giants finished in the cellar did not mean that Marquard would finish the season there with them. In a dramatic development in late August, Rube's career as a Giant came to a crashing halt.

Marquard was sporting a 9–8 record at that point in the season. If there was one man in New York less pleased with Marquard's performance than Marquard, it was McGraw.

McGraw could be a kind and generous man, but he was rarely a subtle one. He began riding Marquard brutally.

"After I'd taken about as much riding as I could stand," Marquard told Lawrence Ritter in 1966 in *The Glory of Their Times*, "I asked him to trade me if he thought I was so bad."

"Who would have you?" McGraw answered.

"I can lick any club in the league," Rube shot back.

"You couldn't," McGraw answered in his usual charming fashion, "lick a postage stamp."

"We were both pretty mad," Rube would always remember. But the gauntlets were down. McGraw put Marquard on waivers, but—suspiciously—he went unclaimed. It was as if no one believed the waivers, or McGraw had passed the word around the league not to claim him.

Rube then requested the opportunity to trade or sell himself. McGraw wanted $7,500, a price that, in retrospect, he probably figured was prohibitively high.

Two days later, Marquard appeared in his manager's office. Rube was still angry. And he wanted to pursue the point of his value. McGraw, after all, was now making noises about sending Rube to Newark of the International League for the rest of the season. From the bright lights of Broadway to Newark was not a prospect that Rube looked upon with favor.

"Let me use your phone," Marquard asked.

As McGraw stood by and watched, Marquard phoned his old coach Wilbert Robinson in Brooklyn.

"How would you like a left-handed pitcher?" Rube asked.

"Who?" Robinson answered.

"Me," said Rube.

Once Uncle Robbie understood that this was not a hoax, he leaped at the opportunity. The deal was made that afternoon. The date was August 26, 1915. Rube Marquard was no longer a New York Giant. Though McGraw would make a halfhearted attempt to get Marquard back within the year, Rube was gone from the club for good.

Though liberated from McGraw's tyranny, this was not a particularly happy time for Rube. He would be 2–2 for the Robins in the final weeks of the season with a porcine ERA of 6.12. Not yet twenty-six years old, two aspects of his life seemed to be falling apart.

He was no longer an effective pitcher, or at least he hadn't been for the last two seasons. And his marriage was hitting the rocks almost as abruptly.

In public, Rube and Blossom made a display of their affection for each other. They used their highly visible marriage for whatever publicity served their purposes. And Rube made a good show of being a father by taking his son to the ballpark, particularly in Brooklyn, and letting the boy hang out in the dugout, particularly for photographers.

But the relationship between Rube and Blossom had crashed upon a difference that quickly became irreconcilable.

"I asked Blossom to quit the stage," Rube said years later, encapsulating many long discussions with his wife, a debate that raged for two years in their marriage. "I told her I could give her everything that she wanted."

"No," Blossom answered continually. "Show business is show business."

Rube may have thought that he could have given his wife everything she wanted, but he had missed one great point—one which ironically he should have been in a position to understand.

Just as he could never give up the thrill of taking the mound in a packed ballpark and staring down—then shutting down—the opposing team, Blossom could never pull herself away from the excitement of the stage. Performance—sporting and theatrical—had been in the blood of both Rube and Blossom since their respective childhoods. Theatergoers in San Francisco and Los Angeles would always remember Little Blossom, the child star, just as old firemen and ballplayers on Cleveland's West Side would always remember a kid called Ritchie LeMarquis who always had a baseball in his hand, flipping it in a tattered glove, dirty hat crooked on his head, looking for whatever game might break out.

Years later when these two personalities finally came

together as adults, the dynamics of their two careers were more than the marriage could stand. The love affair that had been born in passion, scandal, and bright footlights, could not survive each partner's request for the other to give up his or her career.

"Well," Rube remembered finally telling his wife. "Show business is your career. But baseball is mine."

It was almost that easy. Or at least that's how Rube made it sound.

"So we separated," Rube recalled half a century later.

By 1916, the marriage was effectively over.

16

Professionally at least, Rube landed on his feet in 1916. Playing for the Robins, Marquard found a spot in Wilbert Robinson's pitching rotation as a fourth starter and occasional reliever. Rube thrived under the circumstances, going 13–8 with an ERA of 1.62. Much to the amazement of everyone in baseball, the Robins shot past the rest of the National League and brought Brooklyn their first pennant of the twentieth century.

A club like this that featured Casey Stengel, Zack Wheat, and Rube Marquard as players, combined with Robinson as the manager, was one that fans had to love. An interesting addition also was Chief Meyers, who had by now been released by the Giants in much the same manner as Marquard. Born again with Uncle Robbie, the Chief became the starting catcher for the Robins and turned in a creditable year.

The World Series was a different story.

The American League champions were the Boston Red Sox, following the sparks ignited by their star pitcher and hitter, Babe Ruth. Ruth, now twenty-one, won twenty-three games that season and had quickly become the top left-handed pitcher in baseball, a position that Rube had occupied five short years ago. Marquard couldn't have missed that detail.

Marquard started Game One and the Red Sox got to him quickly, as they did with all the Robins' pitchers that October, winning the series in five games. Rube came away with two losses for the series and Ruth pitched a fourteen-inning gem in Game Two. The only Brooklyn player to have a respectable series was Casey Stengel—the Loquacious One hit .364 in the losing effort.

After the series, Blossom went on her usual fall tour. She and her husband put their differences aside for a short time and Rube came along. He was frequently cornered by reporters who wanted to talk about baseball.

Sometimes following a Seeley performance, if Rube was traveling with her, the audience would shout, "Rube! Rube!" demanding that Marquard at least give them a wave from offstage or from his seat in the audience. This had to have grated upon Seeley, who was a female headliner of the first rank during this time and who didn't much care for being defined by who her husband was. But she never publicly said a negative word on the subject. What she said in private was another matter, and by 1917 Rube was no longer traveling with her.

In the fall of 1917, Rube took a final spin at vaudeville, himself, following a season in which he returned to his old form and won nineteen games for Brooklyn. He worked a "two" act with a famous but runtish Philadelphia actor named William Dooley. Marquard and Dooley presented a seventeen-minute skit defined as "songs, dances, and comedy." All three elements were essentially handled by Dooley.

The act played the Palace due to the fame of both participants. It was Rube's last grasp at show business. No mention was made of baseball. Obviously, Rube — who was the straight man to the "rough comedy" of Dooley — wanted to see how he could do without Blossom and whether — in the manner of Mike Donlin — he had a future career in show biz even without Blossom.

This time, the critics had the scalpels out. And they answered his question for him.

"Only once did Rube show any speed," remarked *Variety*.

"Dooley carries the act," commented the *New York Telegraph*.

Other publications were even less kind, and the verdict was quickly in. Aside from a few lesser flirtations, and a career as a speaker and a storyteller, Marquard and vaudeville were finished with each other. Meanwhile, on competing bills across town, Blossom was knocking audiences out without having to listen to the tiresome "Rube, Rube," chorus at the close of her act.

So Rube returned to baseball and the Robins. He pitched well there for five full seasons, not withstanding a broken leg in 1919.

And one day, after more than a decade of silence, his father turned up in the Brooklyn clubhouse to end the long feud that had begun when Rube had run away to become a ballplayer. For years, the elder LeMarquis hadn't even known that the famous Rube Marquard of the Giants was his son. In the Brooklyn locker room one day after a game, the two men tearfully buried their old grievances.

Rube also helped lead Brooklyn to another pennant in 1920, whereupon—just to show that he could never completely stay away from controversy—he took a final and again-unwelcome turn in the national spotlight.

By the autumn of 1920, the U.S. was in the midst of another Presidential election. Woodrow Wilson was ailing gravely from a paralytic stroke suffered in September 1919. Associated illnesses and infirmities would take Wilson's life in another four years. Currently, Mrs. Wilson was silently running the country.

The American voters had a choice between Charles Dawes and Warren Harding and would, within another month, use their inestimable wisdom to choose the latter.

The sports world had its own focus. Jack Dempsey, who had won the heavyweight championship on July 4, 1919, defended his title for the first time on September 6, 1920. He had little trouble with challenger Billy Miske, knocking out Miske in three rounds in Benton Harbor, Michigan. Ominously, however, the sports pages and the news pages remained full of the rumor and innuendo about the supposed fix of the 1919 World Series. The story broke fully in September. Up until then, the White Sox had seemed destined to repeat as American League champions, though they were involved in a hot pennant race with both the New York Yankees and the Cleveland Indians.

But on September 28, when the newspapers broke the story of the alleged fix of the 1919 World Series, Commissioner Landis immediately suspended the seven tainted current White Sox, plus Chick Gandil, who had actually retired following the previous World Series. The suspensions, with only days left in the season, were enough to tip the American League pennant to the Cleveland Indians. And it was almost enough to throw a pall over the Series of 1920.

Cleveland ended up winning the American League pennant by two games over Chicago and three games over the newly resurgent New York Yankees. In truth, the Yankees of 1920 were the club of baseball's future, and that year they served notice that baseball would never be quite the same.

In his first year as a Yankee in 1920, Ruth had hit an incomprehensible total of fifty-four home runs. And as fans flocked to the Polo Grounds, where the Yankees played as the tenants of the Giants, it was clear to see that in the post-World War I America, fans wanted to see this new "TNT ball" that John McGraw so disparaged. McGraw had seen the future and didn't much like it. But he also couldn't do much about it, other than eventually making plans to evict the Yankees to some obscure real estate in the Bronx. That Cleveland, managed and fueled by a classic dead ballplayer like Tris Speaker, hung on to win a championship only showed that the old order died slowly. An interesting contrast: Ruth hit fifty-four home runs, and the league champion Indians hit a team total of thirty-five.

Not that the Indians were a bad club. Speaker presided over a solid lineup, yet was his own best player, hitting .388. He had a gaping hole at shortstop, following the tragic death of Ray Chapman who had been beaned by Yankee Carl Mays on August 16 at the Polo Grounds. But twenty-two-year-old Joe Sewell, brought up from the minors in September, finally filled the breach. Speaker also had a trio of front line pitchers—Jim Bagby, Stan Coveleskie, and Ray Caldwell—who won seventy-five of the club's ninety-eight victories that year.

But in many ways, this was the swan song for old-time baseball in the American League. Within another year, the White Sox stars would be gone for good and the Yankees would have written out enough checks to buy players from the Boston Red Sox to tip the balance of power in the American League for the next forty-five years. Even the fine Connie Mack teams of the 1920s and 1930s that challenged, and sometimes outdistanced, the Yankees, would incorporate slugging into their attack.

Back in the National League, the Brooklyn club won their second pennant of the modern era in 1920, coming home seven full games ahead of the Giants. Rube was still a spot starter on the club and turned in a solid year for a flaky lefty who had just celebrated his thirtieth birthday. Rube was 10–7 and pitched solidly most of the season, his best campaign since the 19–12 season of 1917.

The World Series had switched back to its original best-of-nine format in 1919 and continued in that cumbersome form in 1920. The first three games were to be played in Brooklyn, the middle four in Cleveland where—as fate would have it — Rube's parents still lived and where his seven-year-old son — living temporarily with Rube's parents — was in school. The final two games, should they be necessary, were scheduled for Brooklyn.

Rube pitched the first game of the series and pitched well, but was bested 3–1 by Stan Coveleskie, the great right-hander from Shamokin, Pennsylvania. Rube deserved better, as two unearned runs beat him. Burleigh Grimes won the second game for the Robins and Sherry Smith won the third, sending the series to the Forest City for Game Four, Brooklyn up, 2–1.

If there was a last great "spitball world series," this was it, as Grimes and Coveleskie were two of the masters of the wet science, which would soon be banned from the major leagues by Judge Landis. Grimes had the charming habit of licking the ball directly with his tongue to add moisture to his pitching formula. Coveleskie, a more refined man, would spit into his palm and rub the ball.

Naturally, Rube was returning to Cleveland in triumph. He was the local boy who had both made good and made headlines in his heyday with the Giants. Naturally, he was able to spend time with his family and received visits from swarms of friends as he returned to his hometown. And just as naturally, Rube couldn't stay out of trouble. Or the headlines.

Ensconced in a fashionable hotel in his native city, Marquard spent a few minutes in the hotel lobby on the morning of Game Four, attempting to unload his set of box seat tickets for a profit. Marquard spotted what appeared to be a sucker and offered him the seats for $350.

Unfortunately, Rube's judgment wasn't much better than his pitch selections had been to Frank Baker in 1911. Marquard's "sucker" was an undercover Cleveland cop who was in the lobby — you guessed it — trying to snare ticket scalpers.

Rube was busted with seven other professional scalpers and suffered the indignity of being hustled off to the gendarmerie. There, somewhat befuddled, he announced who he was to a surprised booking officer. The situation filtered up the chain of command of the Cleveland Police until Police Chief Michael Smith personally allowed Marquard to be released until after the day's game, at which time Rube promised he would return to the police station.

"Under the circumstances, we could not delay Marquard from reporting to the ballpark," Chief Smith told newspapermen. "That would have been unsportsmanlike."

Then again, if Chief Smith was an Indian fan, he might have known what he was doing, for Rube was snakebit against the Tribe.

Marquard hustled out to League Park where Uncle Robbie was less than happy to hear about his pitcher's bout with the police that morning. Following the horrible publicity generated by the Black Sox scandal, which remained in the forefront of the news, the last thing any club wanted was a player spending the morning in the police station. And once the game began, Rube's day did not improve.

Cleveland scored two runs in the first off Brooklyn's

Leon Cadore and chased him in the second inning. Not that Leon wasn't used to pitching longer assignments: his claim to fame will always be pitching the *entire* twenty-six-inning game against Boston the previous May first. Facing Al Mamaux in the third, the Indians quickly put Bill Wambsganss on third and Tris Speaker on second with none out. Uncle Robbie called in Marquard as his third pitcher in less than three innings.

"Don't let the game get out of hand," Uncle Robbie muttered as he turned the ball over to Rube.

Rube promptly yielded a single to George Burns that scored both runners and allowed the game to do just that. The Indians went on to win the game, 5-1. Marquard actually pitched quite well, yielding no runs himself, and allowing only two hits and a walk over three innings.

Meanwhile, as word circulated through the city of Marquard's arrest, the tall lefty quickly became the most talked about player in the series. So far. The next day, Sunday, October 10, Marquard was arraigned in municipal court on a charge of "violation of the exhibition ordinance." Rube entered a plea of not guilty and left the courthouse with a crowd of reporters around him. At the ballpark that afternoon, Marquard found himself firmly entrenched in his manager's doghouse. So he sat on the bench and could only watch in wonder at the unique game that followed.

Indian right-fielder Elmer Smith hit the first-ever grand slam in World Series history in the first inning. Then, trailing 7-0, in the fifth inning the Robins looked to have a potential rally going—two men on, none out—

when pitcher Clarence Mitchell came to bat. Mitchell was a good hitter who, over the course of an eighteen-year career, also occasionally played the outfield and first base. It was not unusual that he would bat for himself. What *was* unusual was what happened.

Mitchell lined a 1–1 pitch toward center field. Everyone in the park thought it was a hit, including second baseman Bill Wambsganss, owner of one of baseball's most unique names. Wambsganss took three strides from where he was playing, threw his body toward centerfield, and lunged with his glove. Somehow he caught the ball. His momentum took him to second base, where, stepping on the bag, he doubled off Brooklyn runner Pete Kilduff. When Wambsganss turned toward first he saw an astonished Otto Miller standing a few feet away from him. Wambsganss quickly tagged him, completing that rarest of baseball feats, the unassisted triple play, and the only one ever to occur in a World Series.

Marquard had no way of knowing it for sure, but he was finished for this World Series. He would, however, appear in court on Tuesday morning, October 12. There he finally found a friendly soul in one Judge Isaac Silbert.

Marquard, at this point in his life, may have come to expect almost anything when he appeared in a courtroom. But he may have been pleasantly relieved when the judge tossed a little mercy his way.

"I am satisfied that Marquard violated the law and the spirit of the law," spoke the judge. "But I believe he has been punished enough by being written up more than any Presidential candidate. I feel this has been a lesson to him."

Rube's lesson cost him all of three dollars and eighty cents, which included a one dollar fine and—seen in the perspective of years—a quaint two dollars and eighty cents in court costs. After getting his legal problems squared away, Rube bolted for the ballpark where his manager was in a less forgiving mood than the local magistrate.

Marquard, with two good efforts in the series, was the logical stopper for Robinson to go to in Game Seven and give the Robins the chance to take the series back to Brooklyn. But instead, Robinson started Burleigh Grimes again. Grimes pitched well, but not well enough to win. Tris Speaker, seeing a chance to nail shut the Robins coffin, started Stan Coveleskie again, this time on two days' rest.

"Stan," Speaker told Coveleskie before Game Seven, "if you don't win today, you're starting again tomorrow." How was that for a vote of confidence? Whatever it was, it worked. Coveleskie scattered five hits to shut out Brooklyn in Game Seven.

There would be no return to Brooklyn. The Indians had won the World Series, 5–2. The great Coveleskie won three games in the series, the first hurler since Mathewson to do so, and Robins' hitters scored but two runs in the last four games, signaling an impending Brooklyn futility in modern World Series play that would continue another thirty-five years.

For his part, not only did Marquard not appear again in the 1920 World Series after the day of his "scalping" arrest, but he never appeared again in any other. Nor, for that matter, did Rube ever again appear in a Dodger uniform. He had finally worn out his welcome with the normally affable Robinson, his long-ago mentor, who now couldn't wait to unload him. Marquard would be formally traded to Cincinnati for Dutch Reuther in December, but the deal had apparently been agreed to by both clubs weeks earlier.

For years, Marquard insisted that he had been framed in the ticket scalping incident, though Robinson and team owner Charley Ebbets didn't buy the explanation, and wanted Marquard gone from Brooklyn as soon as possible.

"I was waiting for my brother in that hotel lobby," Marquard once told New York sportswriter Dan Daniel. "He was late and I had two tickets for him. Finally, I couldn't wait any longer and I asked the hotel clerk to hold them for him. No sooner did I hand him the tickets than I was grabbed by city detectives. The plot was engineered by an employee of the Cleveland team."

Rube's version of events didn't quite jibe with what the detectives had said, but there were many who believed him. And in any case, the damage was done, fairly or unfairly. The incident ended the goodwill of Brooklyn management toward Marquard. And the public saw Rube as a wealthy man—a celebrity, at that!—trying to grab some extra money when "true fans" couldn't get good seats to the series.

And if October 1920 marked the end of Rube's appearance in the national spotlight in terms of the World Series, it marked the official end of something personal, also.

Shortly after the defeat of the Robins in Game Seven, Blossom Seeley met with her lawyers in Chicago and formally filed suit for divorce. Marquard and Seeley had been separated for more than a year and a half and the grounds she cited were desertion. In truth, the romance and marriage had fizzled out long before that. Rube did not contest the proceeding.

But as was frequently the case, Blossom was thinking not just about her past, but also her future. In Chicago recently she had met a then small-time entertainer in a lounge named Benny Fields. Seeley and Fields struck romantic and professional sparks right away. Seeley, the headliner, had taken the unknown singer and comedian into her act.

Seeley and Fields, they would be called.

In 1921, they would also be married. Hence, the necessary divorce decree against Rube at the end of 1920.

EPILOGUE

Not surprisingly, Marquard and Seeley, even after going their respective ways, were never far from the spotlight.

Charlie Ebbets, true to his word, had made sure that Marquard never pitched again for the Brooklyn club. But there were still some wins in Rube's arm. The very next year, for example, Rube won seventeen games for sixth-place Cincinnati.

The Reds then showed their gratitude by trading Rube again, this time to the Boston Braves in February 1922 for journeymen Jack Scott and Larry Kopf. At that point, at age thirty-two, Rube was finally on his way down as a major league pitcher. He never again had a winning major league season and never again won more than eleven games in a year. Appendicitis virtually ended his career as a big leaguer in 1924. By that time he had won 201 games in sixteen major league seasons. He had also pitched in eleven games in five World Series.

And still he hung around the game.

Between 1926 and 1932, he pitched in the high minors. He also managed — Providence in the Eastern

League in 1926 and Jacksonville in the Southeastern League in 1929 and 1930.

He even took an uncomfortable stint as an umpire in the Eastern League in 1931, before making an unsuccessful six-game appearance as a pitcher with Atlanta in the Southern Association in 1932. By that time, Rube was forty-three years old and should have known better.

He married a woman named Naomi Wigley in 1921 and remained married to her for thirty-three years, until her death in 1954. The next year he married for the third and final time, a Jane Ottenheimer. His only child was with Blossom.

After Rube's baseball career ended, he became a parimutuel clerk for many years at racetracks in Florida, Maryland, New Jersey and Rhode Island, though he remained a Baltimore resident from 1930 on. He also had a pretty good career at being Rube Marquard, an accessible, talkative interview for anyone who wanted to chat about baseball in the old days.

Writers loved him. There is no mystery why Lawrence Ritter chose Marquard's interview to be the keynote chapter of *The Glory of Their Times*.

When the New York Giants moved west after the 1957 season, and departed the Polo Grounds forever as a home team, Rube was one of the invitees from the John McGraw era to be present at the final game. At the time, Christy Mathewson had been dead for thirty-two years and McGraw for twenty-four. It was Marquard and Larry Doyle who were the living links to the past when the old park closed.

Marquard lived to a great age. Born during the administration of Benjamin Harrison, he lived into the year Ronald Reagan became President. In his final years, in his eighties, he continued to be a popular interview. As late as October of 1979, he threw out the ceremonial first ball for his hometown Orioles in a playoff game against the California Angels. And also in the 1970s, his name even surfaced frequently in the sports pages again in conjunction with his most noteworthy accomplishment — nineteen straight wins.

Ron Guidry of the Yankees, another left-hander who threw hard, had won fourteen straight games at the opening of the 1978 season. Previously, Dave McNally of the Orioles and Johnny Allen of the Indians had taken a run at Marquard's single season record with fifteen straight wins at the opening of the season. And another great Giant, Carl Hubbell, had won twenty-six in a row, but over the course of two seasons, 1933 and 1934.

"I've been following the boy," Marquard said from his home in Pikesville, Maryland, referring to Ron Guidry in 1978. "He must be a pretty good pitcher to win all those games."

Guidry was, though his streak stopped at fourteen. But not before Rube sent him a message.

"Give the boy my best," Marquard said, "and wish him well." Most observers seemed to think that Rube was pulling for the young Yankee, despite his pride in his own feat. Then again, Guidry was getting Rube's name back in the papers.

Guidry's streak stopped at fourteen. Eight years later,

a Roger Clemens streak also stopped at fourteen. No one has come close since. Modern players take runs at Joe DiMaggio's consecutive game hitting streak more often than Marquard's nineteen straight wins. Eighty-three years later, no one has eclipsed Rube Marquard's record.

In some ways, Blossom Seeley even surpassed the fame and success of her second husband.

Seeley first found Benny Fields performing as part of trio in a third-rate Chicago nightclub.

"I hired him and his two partners," she later told friends, "because I fell instantly in love with the big lug the minute I saw him. I favored him in the act until his two partners quit. Then I had Benny to myself."

Blossom always stayed far ahead of her time, and always seemed to know what she wanted. And how to get it.

Fields became her accompanist, managing her music, wardrobe, and sets. She was a star at the time and he was — as they both later recalled it — "a nobody." Fields was derisively known in vaudeville circles as "Mr. Blossom Seeley." And friends predicted that Blossom's marriage to Fields would last a far shorter time than the one to Marquard.

But just as headlines had always seemed to follow Marquard and Seeley, they also followed Seeley and Fields.

Once, after finishing a week in Boston, Seeley and Fields were to take a midnight train to New York. At the last minute, they changed their plans and took a later train.

The train they had meant to take was derailed in Rhode Island in a massive accident. Several people died. The next evening in New York, Seeley and Fields walked into Lindy's Restaurant for dinner. The headwaiter turned white when he saw them.

Then he showed them the headlines on a newspaper. One journal in New England had jumped the gun on the story and had gone to press with a rumor. Other members of the media had picked it up.

The headline read,

BLOSSOM SEELEY DIES IN PROVIDENCE

Seeley stared at it and didn't miss a beat.

"Well, I *never!*" she exclaimed. "Died in Providence? They always *loved* me there!"

Another time, Seeley and Fields were playing the Orpheum in Memphis. Just after they left the theater one evening, the building caught fire. When Seeley and Fields rushed back to the theater to save their sets, costumes, and music, they noticed the marquee:

BLOSSOM SEELEY — THE HOTTEST
GAL IN TOWN

In the next city they visited, Fields had Blossom billed as, "So hot she burned the theater down in Memphis."

During the 1920s, Blossom toured constantly with both Fields and the "hottest girl in town" label.

The latter was hardly an overstatement. Blossom remained a headliner through that decade, working the Keith-Albee-Orpheum circuit even as it struggled against the inroads that motion pictures—silents and eventually talkies—made against vaudeville. The "hot" accolade was a tribute to Blossom's smoldering renditions of several very popular signature songs: "Somebody Loves Me," which George Gershwin wrote especially for her, "Jealous," "Smiles," "I Cried for You," and "Way Down Yonder In New Orleans." All of these tunes became closely associated with her name. Then, in 1927, Seeley and Fields were selected to headline a bill at the Palace to commemorate the purported 100th anniversary of vaudeville.

In the 1930s, Seeley and Fields hit more difficult times, but not for the predictable reasons.

Fields tired of being known as "the headliner's husband." In his own right he was a talented singer, dancer, and musician. Seeley, now in her forties and on her third marriage, was in no way inclined to see her way through another painful divorce. Once again, she had to make a decision between her career and her marriage. This time, she chose her marriage.

"It was during the worst of the Depression," Blossom later explained. "I told Benny that I wanted to retire. From then on, *he* was the one who would have to do the singing. I would help if I could, but it was up to him to earn our living."

These were not easy times. Newspapers printed stories of Fields and Seeley in bankruptcy or Blossom taking jewelry to pawnshops to meet expenses. The stories were true, at least in part. Seeley went from a headliner to invisible almost overnight. But she felt that this situation had to take place before her husband could attain the stardom he deserved.

It turned out that she was right.

Around 1936, Benny Fields suddenly clicked and *he* became a headliner. Fields's success brought Blossom back into the public eye, albeit as a supporting player to her husband. The couple later starred on their own radio show in the 1940s and, inevitably, a Hollywood film titled *Somebody Loves Me* was made about their lives together.

In the film, Betty Hutton played Blossom Seeley. Ralph Meeker played Benny Fields. Rube Marquard and Joe Kane (who also remarried in 1917) did not even rate a mention. The 1952 film was successful enough to spark yet a "second comeback" for Seeley and Fields. They even played Las Vegas. Then, after thirty-six years of marriage, Benny Fields died in 1959. Seven years later, Blossom made her last public appearance on the *Ed Sullivan Show* in 1966.

One wonders what Joe Kane would have thought and said about all this. But Joe had no way of commenting, having died in show biz obscurity — also known as Wisconsin — on April 30, 1933.

Marquard and Seeley were each married three times, the final marriage being the most enduring for both of them. Blossom lived the final years of her life on the East Side of Manhattan. And to the surprise of everyone, she kept up a written correspondence with Marquard for half a century after their divorce.

"Richard's a wonderful man," Blossom told Al Ellenberg of the *New York Post* in 1971. "We're still very affectionate."

By the same token, Marquard, whenever Blossom's name was raised by visiting writers, would always refer to her as "a wonderful lady." There was never an ill word of one from the other that any friend could remember. Obviously, the memories were splendid. And the rancor and hurt of their divorce had long faded.

But Rube Marquard and Blossom Seeley belonged to a particular time, place, and generation that has long since passed. The New York Giants are a distant memory to most Americans and vaudeville—even the concept of vaudeville—is even more remote. And with their time and generation, Marquard and Seeley have also long since passed from the scene.

Blossom died first, in a New York nursing home on April 17, 1974. She was eighty-two years old. Or so she would have had you believe.

Rube Marquard was the oldest living member of baseball's Hall of Fame until death claimed him on June 1, 1980. He was ninety years old. He would have been pleased at his obituary in the *New York Times*, which, in its headline, mentioned "Hall of Fame," "19 in a Row," and "Involved in Scandal."

At the time of Rube's passing, sixty-five years had passed since he had last taken the stage with Blossom. Sixty years had passed since their marriage had ended. Like the theaters they played as a "mixed act," and like the ballparks where Rube's powerful left arm had won him his greatest successes, their partnership was a thing of only legend and, to a very few, a dim distant memory.

But as a team—and in the brilliance and passion of their youths—Marquard and Seeley had performed to packed houses and cheering, enthralled audiences.

And together, for three fleeting years, they had been among the brightest stars their nation had ever produced.

BIBLIOGRAPHY

BOOKS

Alexander, Charles C. *Ty Cobb.* New York: Oxford University Press, 1984.

_____. *John McGraw.* New York: Viking, 1988.

Allen, Lee. *The National League Story.* New York: Hill & Wang, 1961.

Connor, Anthony J. *Voices From Cooperstown.* New York: Macmillan, 1982.

Graham, Frank. *McGraw of The Giants.* New York: Putnam, 1944.

Gutman, Dan. *Baseball Babylon.* New York: Penguin, 1992

Hynd, Alan. *The Cherry Sisters.* Published in *The American Mercury,* New York, August 1950.

Hynd, Noel. *The Giants of The Polo Grounds.* New York: Doubleday & Co., 1988.

Laurie, Joe, Jr. *VAUDEVILLE From the Honky Tonks to The Palace*. New York: Henry Holt & Co., 1953.

Laurie, Joe, Jr. and Green, Abel. *Show Biz*. New York: Henry Holt & Co., 1951.

Mathewson, Christy. *Pitching In a Pinch*. New York: Putnam, 1912.

McGraw, John J. *My Thirty Years in Baseball*. New York: Boni & Liveright, 1923.

McGraw, Mrs. John J. *The Real McGraw*. New York: David McKay, 1953.

Morris, Lloyd. *Incredible New York*. New York: Random House, 1951.

Ritter, Lawrence. *The Glory of Their Times*. New York: Macmillan, 1966.

Rubin, Benny. *Come Backstage With Me*. Bowling Green, Ohio: Bowling Green University Press, 1957.

Salant, Richard. *Superstars, Stars and Just Plain Heroes*. New York: Stein and Day, 1982.

Seymour, Harold. *Baseball: The Golden Age*. New York: Oxford University Press, 1971.

Snyder, Robert W. *The Voice of The City: Vaudeville and Popular Culture in New York*. New York: Oxford University Press, 1989.

Sowell, Mike. *The Pitch That Killed*. New York: Macmillan, 1989.

Stein, Fred, and Nick Peters. *Giants Diary*. Berkeley, California: North Atlantic Books, 1987.

NEWSPAPERS

New York American	1908–1921
New York Times	1908–1921, 1974, 1980
New York Tribune	1908–1921
New York Telegraph	1908–1921
New York Post	1980
The Sporting News	1900–1980
Variety	1900–1980

The author welcomes readers' questions and comments on *Marquard & Seeley* either via the publisher or directly through electronic mail. Noel Hynd can be reached at NHy1212@AOL.com.